FEAR NO FOE

FEAR NO FOE

A Brother's Story

John Pollock

Hodder & Stoughton

LONDON SYDNEY AUCKLAND

The portrait on the front cover was specially painted for this book by Hugh Powell, Michael's cousin. They served together at Sandhurst, then Hugh saw action in Burma, the Middle East and Italy. After the war he became a distinguished designer of stained glass, having completed over 100 commissions for windows in this country, the Channel Islands and Canada, and over 200 portraits, including Sir John Loveridge, the Bailiff of Guernsey, John Habgood, now Archbishop of York and Dame Margot Fonteyn.

British Library Cataloguing in Publication Data
A catalogue record for this book is available from the British Library.

ISBN 0-340-55806-7

Published by Hodder and Stoughton,
a division of Hodder and Stoughton Ltd,
Mill Road, Dunton Green, Sevenoaks, Kent TN13 2YA
Editorial Office: 47 Bedford Square, London WC1B 3DP.

Typeset by Hewer Text Composition Services, Edinburgh.
Printed in Great Britain by Clays Ltd, St Ives plc.

**In Memory of
Michael
and of
Stanley, Coldstream Guards,
Belgium, 1944,
and
Derek, 60th Rifles,
Germany, 1945**

'I fear no foe with thee at hand to bless;
Ills have no weight, and tears no bitterness.
Where is death's sting? Where, grave, thy victory?
I triumph still, if thou abide with me.'

H. F. Lyte, 1793–1847
'Abide with me'

List of Illustrations

Michael with his parents, Summer 1940.[1]
Officers of "A" Squadron, Tilford, December 1940.[2]
Churchill with the Bays, inspecting a Honey tank, August 1941.[3]
The Colonel-in-Chief's Farewell, 17th September 1941.[3]
Part of a letter from Michael.

Captain Tom Butler-Stoney, MC, RHA[4]
The badge of the Queen's Bays.[3]
The Bays' first khamsin.[5]
Brewing up, desert style.[5]
Map of the Msus Stakes, January 1942.[6]
Sermon on the sand.[3]
Holy Communion in the desert.[7]
Into Action: the Bays advance at the Battle of Gazala.[5]

Acknowledgments

[1] Photo: Mr M.J. Pollock.
[2] Photo courtesy of Major D.F. McCallan.
[3] Photo courtesy of Mr J.M.G. Halsted.
[4] Photo courtesy of Mr R.H. Butler-Stoney.
[5] Photo: Mr H. Havge.
[6] Map taken from *A History of the Queen's Bays, 1929–45.*
[7] Photo courtesy of the Rev Prebendary J.B. Morson.

Contents

Acknowledgements

Relatives, friends and comrades of Michael gave me information and memories. I am grateful to them all and especially to the late Colonel G. W. C. Draffen DSO, and many of all ranks who served under his command in the Queen's Bays, 1940–42. They, and their Padre, the Reverend Prebendary J. B. Morson OBE, MC, TD, shared with me their memories of Michael, and of the Convoy and the North African campaign, and guided me in matters relating to the Regiment.

Among them I would particularly like to thank Major D. F. MacCallan and Mr J. M. G. Halsted OBE. Douglas MacCallan encouraged and guided me all along, and Michael Halsted, very happily for me, published his wartime diary just before I started work on my final draft. His *Shots in the Sand: An Undergraduate Goes to War* (Gooday Publishers, East Wittering, West Sussex, 1990) covers many of the events which Michael Pollock lived through, although from a slightly different angle as they were not in the same squadron. It is a vivid and detailed contemporary account, an important contribution to the literature of the campaign. Mr Halsted kindly allowed me to quote from his book; he read part of my draft and answered many questions.

I would like to thank General Sir Jack Harman GCB, OBE, MC (once Michael's Squadron Leader) and

Lieutenant-General Sir Maurice Johnston KCB, OBE, DL, successive Honorary Colonels of the 1st Queen's Dragoon Guards, successor Regiment to the Queen's Bays; and the secretaries of the Regimental Association in 1968 (Lieutenant Colonel A. Rowland OBE, MC) and in 1991 (Major K. McMillan). *A History of the Queen's Bays 1929–1945* by Major-General W. R. Beddington CBE (Warren & Son, Winchester, 1954) has been very useful, and I am grateful for permission to reproduce a map.

For guidance on medical matters I am grateful to Lord Richardson LVO, MD, FRCP. For supplying or helping to locate photographs I am indebted to the kindness of Home Headquarters, 1st Queen's Dragoon Guards, Mr Richard Butler-Stoney, Major Douglas MacCallan, Major Peter Gill, Mr Michael Halsted, Mr Herman Hauge, the Reverend Prebendary Basil Morson, Mr Martin Pollock, and Mr Ian Wallace, OBE. I thank Mrs J. E. Williams of Bideford, North Devon, who skilfully typed yet another of my books.

My editor at Hodder and Stoughton, Miss Carolyn Armitage, and her team have been most helpful, as also Miss Juliet Newport, late of Hodders.

Finally I want to give warmest thanks to my cousin Hugh Powell MGP, one of Michael's close friends, now a distinguished portrait painter, and designer of stained glass, for his magnificent portrait of Michael, painted specially for this book. My first sight of it quite bowled me over. Hugh had placed it at head height. I entered his studio to find Michael 'standing' there, just as I had known him.

John Pollock
Rose Ash
Devonshire

Prologue

Desert Clash

Dawn in the Western Desert broke clear but cold on 25 January 1942. As he shook himself awake beside his tank, an order came to twenty-two-year-old Lieutenant Michael Pollock, Queen's Bays – my next elder brother and dearest friend – to take his own and another tank to join a composite force a short distance away.

The battle had already lasted two days and had not gone to plan. The Queen's Bays, in North Africa for only a month, had crossed six hundred miles of desert with the 1st Armoured Division to join the victorious Eighth Army which had relieved Tobruk and thrown Rommel's Afrika Korps out of Cyrenaica: the Bays expected to be in at the final push which would defeat him and clear the North African shore.

But it was Rommel who was pushing. Unknown to the Higher Command he had been heavily reinforced and had poured through a gap in the British forward divisions, and now was swirling around the reserve. Two days earlier Michael's Regiment 'had had our first taste of action – not that we'd accomplished anything – and the whole thing was a little bewildering at first.' Even after the second day of the battle they thought they were opposed by small forces 'and sooner or later we'd just surround them or shell them out.'

Unlike their successors in the 'Desert Storm' nearly fifty years later, the 1st Armoured Division of 1942 had no high technological precision air strikes to prepare their way, or to call up when attacked; nor satellite intelligence. Even the closely guarded, top secret Ultra intelligence, which none below Army command knew about, had failed or been misinterpreted.

Front line units were out on their own, but the Bays had a first rate Colonel and were a closely knit Regiment with a high degree of mutual trust between all ranks.

When the order came, Michael and his two-man crew jumped into their light American tank (officially a Stuart but they were always known as Honeys). Michael just had time to glance at his pocket Bible anthology, *Daily Light*, for January 25: 'I count all things but loss for the excellency of the knowledge of Christ Jesus my Lord,' he read; and he knew that it was 'the excellency of the knowledge of Christ' which had made his life joyful these past fifteen months, and which gave him assurance now.

His driver revved the engine and they raced through the sand to the composite force, commanded by a charming major from another regiment 'who wore a large Australian hat'. Michael thought that nothing much would happen that morning, especially as the Germans on the higher ground had the sun in their eyes, 'but no sooner had we opened out fanwise than the Germans opened fire from their hill and several columns were seen to be moving.'

The wireless crackled and Michael's operator-gunner passed an order from the major in the Australian hat: to investigate some German self-propelled anti-tank guns believed to be moving on the other side of the ridge. Michael told his driver to proceed at speed under cover of a ridge. With a quick, silent prayer for skill for all three, to 'the Lord, my refuge and my fortress', Michael stood in the turret, sweeping the ground with his field-glasses as the tank rumbled forward.

When the Honey came over the ridge, a German anti-tank gunner and Michael saw each other simultaneously and fired. The German shell hit the tank with a tremendous shock, but only penetrated the driver's steel flap: fired a second later, or at six inches' difference in angle, and all three in the tank would have been seriously wounded or killed, since a German 88 mm shell would have pierced the steel. The driver was unhurt; and Michael's gunner was sure he had scored a hit on the German.

Soon after this, the wireless crackled again. Michael was ordered to withdraw with the Bays and the composite force. That night, as he lay down under the stars after further manoeuvres and much hostile gunfire, but no harm, he fell asleep thanking God for protection.

Nearly five months later Michael was wounded in the head by a bomb splinter on the last day but one of the Battle of Gazala near Tobruk, and evacuated unconscious to Cairo.

He had never thought that God's protection meant a charmed life; rather that nothing could happen unless it were part of what Michael called 'the Great Plan'.

One of his favourite verses in the Bible, which he had both underlined and pencilled in capitals at the top of the page in his pocket New Testament, was St Paul's statement, the birthright of every Christian: 'To me, to

live is Christ and to die is gain' (Philippians 1: 21). Jesus
Christ, through his Spirit, had become Michael's closest
Friend fifteen months earlier, and (as Paul said) death
would be 'to depart and be with Christ'. Michael loved
life for he had a most happy nature, but he knew he
would continue to enjoy this Friendship wherever he
was, on earth or in heaven.

A fortnight after he was wounded, Michael was
writing again. His letters from a hospital bed were
as full and amusing, and clear to read, as any he had
written from the Desert to our parents, to whom he was
devoted. Michael was a natural writer, and moreover
in his letters to me he had described and explored the
implications of his Christian faith with great openness.
Our correspondence had flourished; in some ways my
own career as a writer had already received its first
impetus through Michael, nearly two years before.

Early in August 1942 I was down at Iwerne Minster
in Dorset helping at a farming camp for schoolboys: I
was a Cambridge undergraduate, aged eighteen, before
being called up to the army. At breakfast one morning
I opened a letter from my mother and was shocked
to read: 'How shall I tell you that our darling Michael
has gone to be with the Saviour he loved so well?' The
wound to his head had healed outwardly but all was
not well. The surgeons had needed to perform a second
operation, during which he died.

I took the letter to the Camp commandant, a wise
and gentle clergyman in early middle-age whose quiet
influence on our generation, and indeed on Michael,
was great. We went into an empty room. I could see
that he shared my grief, for even had he not known
Michael he understood the young; but he made a
surprising remark, which helped me far more than

conventional condolence. Speaking in a way which reached across to my sorrow and shock, he said: 'John, it's like having a tooth out. It hurts like mad. But time is the healer – it really is. You don't have to worry about Michael. You know he is with the Lord and you'll meet again. But if you go around being sorry for yourself you won't be able to do your work as a Camp officer.'

I saw his point at once. A door clanged shut in my brain. Michael was in the past, the Lord was in the present. Michael was as much alive as myself, and I could best honour him by building on his work, not pining for his company. I was able to carry on at Camp and support my parents in our grief.

To blunt the loss I shut his memory to the back of my mind. I never re-read his letters; I made no attempt to visit his grave when I passed briefly through Egypt on war service. His photograph stood on my mantelpiece, but as the decades went by those long-dead heroes whose biographies I wrote were more 'alive' than Michael – until twenty-six years after his death.

I had just finished writing *The Apostle: A Life of Paul*. My wife and I went on holiday to Switzerland, exhausted. A few long walks in the mountains of the High Valais worked wonders. We drove next to Engelberg, then to Grindelwald, and there at the Hotel Belvedere, the night after we had walked to the top of the Faulhorn, I had a vivid dream which left me with extraordinary happiness and peace: I had dreamed about Michael.

Next day, walking above Mürren with the Jungfrau rising clear across the steep valley, I wondered whether I might write a short book about him. I could still remember the vividness of his descriptions of battle and the unaffected way in which he told what the

Lord Jesus meant to him. If Michael had influenced me, perhaps he could influence others.

Back in Devonshire I unearthed the letters. Their effect was astonishing. The years rolled away. Michael stepped right out as if he had died the day before. I could see him, good-looking with a slightly ruddy complexion, firm chin and hazel eyes tinged with blue, and a charming, almost feminine smile. He had light brown, rather silky hair, was slender and fairly tall. His personality had been attractive since earliest years but through the letters I watched again the flowering of a very distinctive Christian character and the deployment of a Christian purpose.

As I read, I was humbled and rebuked. My books about Christian leaders and ordinary disciples, past and present, were getting around the English-speaking world in gratifying quantity, and I had several foreign translations; but Michael's faith and character showed up mine. They led me to fresh repentance and dedication. Soon came a sudden renewal of spiritual force: I felt I would never be the same again.

When I got in touch with those who had served with him, and other friends, I found that the memory remained strong of a happy man they had loved and admired. Yet they knew only a part; much more of Michael springs out from his letters, some of them scribbled beside his tank while waiting for Rommel's attack on the Gazala Line, or between actions during the long, arduous battle which ended in the Fall of Tobruk.

And so I recaptured the delight of his friendship, which one day will be resumed among 'the great multitude, which no man could number'. I wrote a short memoir and circulated it in typescript among those who had known him.

Twenty years on, nearing the fiftieth anniversary of Alamein and the Western Desert battles, and after the nation had again needed to fight a desert war, I felt that I was selfish to keep Michael to myself and his family and friends.

His great potential was cut off by war; he had no opportunity to be well known, but just as the name of the hero of a novel means nothing to the reader before the first page, so I believe that Michael will delight and influence those who never knew him; and he can represent the hundreds of young men who might have been strong Christian leaders, famous in their generation, but who lost their lives in the Second World War. The setting of his true story may be as far away as any historical novel but the themes are eternal and relevant.

Michael was a man of 'honest and good heart', as in the Parable of the Sower. The shelves are crowded with conversion stories of modern equivalents of John Newton, the lecherous young slave trader and blasphemer in the eighteenth century who was converted in a storm at sea, and became the writer of 'Amazing Grace' and other immortal hymns; but young men and women who lead good lives, respected and loved by their contemporaries, need Christ as much as any John Newton. Michael's is a story of the seed which fell on good ground: 'they, which in an honest and good heart, having heard the word, keep it, and bring forth fruit with patience' (Luke 8: 15).

And this book has given me great delight in the writing. One of the privileges of a biographer of Christians is to discover a fresh angle on the Communion of Saints, of the 'whole family in heaven and earth'. His subject becomes his friend; thus Hudson Taylor and

I were 'young men together', for he was thirty-eight when my story stopped, and I was thirty-eight when I wrote it. Lord Shaftesbury, years later, became like a father to me, and despite myself I was reduced to tears as I wrote about his funeral in Westminster Abbey.

When my hero is my own brother and dearest friend, Christian biography becomes a joy to share.

Part One

THIS IS MY FRIEND

'Here might I stay and sing,
   No story so divine;
Never was love, dear King,
   Never was grief like thine.
   This is my Friend,
      In whose sweet praise
      I all my days
   Could gladly spend.'

Samuel Crossman, 1624–84
'My Song is Love Unknown'

1

A Box of Tin Soldiers

In the January before the outbreak of war my parents, Bob and Ethel Pollock, celebrated their silver wedding with a party. The entertainment was a revue written and acted by Michael and myself and Ian Wallace, his closest friend at school, who was already preparing for his celebrated career as a Glyndebourne opera singer and radio and television entertainer. Our elder brother, Martin, stage-managed and our sister, Honor, made the costumes.

It was a glorious occasion and when Michael died of wounds in the Middle East two and a half years later one of the guests wrote to my parents: 'Michael always seemed so amazingly alive, and the last time I saw him was when he and John were acting in the Revue they had written, and he was so completely carried away and loving every minute of it! There was always such a wonderfully happy atmosphere in your home, and you all seemed to adore each other so much.'

Michael and I were inseparable as boys, for although he was nearly four years older than myself, we seemed to meet in the middle, as the younger half of the family. His full names were Robert Michael and he was born

on 21 December 1919 at 13 Chester Street, near Hyde
Park Corner in London.

We lived in a square in the West End of London
where the half-stuccoed houses, each with a digni-
fied porch, looked across to the square garden with
its soot-grimed plane trees. The household coal was
tipped through a manhole in the pavement, and no cars
cluttered the street: they were kept in nearby lock-ups,
and only parked outside when we or our neighbours
were about to drive into the country.

Life in Onslow Square, as in similar parts in the Thirties, was a bridge between the old world of upper-class
England and the new world which would emerge after
the Second World War. The lamplighter came round
with his long pole; occasionally we heard a muffin
man ringing his bell. The organ-grinder regularly took
a pitch in the main street at the end of the square,
where the noisy motor-buses ran. We never saw hunger
marchers or dole queues, and took it for granted that
boys in backstreets had poor clothes, pinched faces
and cockney accents; but my mother, like many of her
friends, did a weekly stint of welfare work, helping at
a crèche in Lambeth.

Children in a South Kensington square were free of
household chores since every home had servants. We
had a married couple who were cook and parlourman
(a parlourman undertook duties despised by a butler,
though after the Staffords left we had a butler who
looked every inch the part, yet would do anything).
There was a housemaid, and an efficient 'between-
maid' who was deaf and dumb; my mother was
teaching her to speak. More important to us than
the others was Nanny Barber, who had come when
Martin was born and stayed to bring us all up.

Nanny was lovable, with a natural dignity and an instinctive way with children: she never had to raise her voice. She was a great teller of stories, mostly about her years with a planter family in Ceylon, and she had a touch of mystery and romance, being fairly sure that her father had been an illegitimate son of a Tichborne, the family of Hampshire baronets and landowners who had been the centre of the famous case of the 'Tichborne Claimant'.

My father was a partner in one of the oldest firms of solicitors in London, which had been founded about 1745; among the firm's clients in the nineteenth century had been the great philanthropist, Lord Shaftesbury. In the morning Daddy would walk the cairn terrier, Simon, round the square garden and then disappear to a rather Dickensian office near the Law Courts, to keep a fatherly eye on the broad acres and maiden aunts of clients up and down the land.

Michael had much of Daddy's character: kind-hearted, tolerant and always cheerful and quick to laugh. Daddy was an even better raconteur than Nanny. His heart was in the country, especially in field sports and horsemanship, and in racing and golf, but Michael preferred cricket.

Unlike Daddy, Michael was musical, taking after Mummy, who sang in the Bach Choir and other choirs, whereas Daddy might occasionally burst into a tuneless rendering of old music-hall ditties. The children divided evenly, the two elder being unmusical, while Michael and I both loved Gilbert and Sullivan and classical music. With his long tapering fingers – double-jointed, to his amusement – Michael would play by ear or improvise on the cottage piano in the nursery; we did not touch the drawing-room grand. Neither of us mastered four-part sight reading, despite lessons, but Michael took up the clarinet and, later, timpani.

If music was a part of the atmosphere of home, so was history. A print of our great-great-uncle, Field Marshal Sir George Pollock, who forced the Khyber Pass in 1842, hung on the stairs, and a portrait of our great-grandfather when Attorney-General in the government of Sir Robert Peel, hung in the alcove. Long ago the Pollocks had lived for generations as barons of land near Glasgow, having come to Scotland from Shropshire in the twelfth century with Walter Fitzalan, ancestor of the Stewart kings. The family crest, a boar pierced by a dart, was granted before 1208 for saving the life of a king of Scotland from a ferocious wild boar.

In the late seventeenth century the younger son of a cadet branch, Pollock of Balgray, had moved to the Border country where he was a yeoman farmer. His grandson, David, a saddler, migrated south to London and set up shop at Charing Cross, becoming sadler to King George III and the royal Dukes, who nearly ruined him by not paying their bills.

David Pollock, the sadler, had three remarkable sons. The eldest, Sir David, was both scientist and lawyer, a founder of the Gas Light and Coke Company, Fellow of the Royal Society, and eventually Chief Justice of Bombay. The second, Sir Frederick, our great-grandfather, was a mathematician and lawyer, becoming Attorney-General, and then a judge as Lord Chief Baron of the Exchequer for twenty-two years; the third was the field marshal. A more recent parallel comes with the Dennings, where a Hampshire grocer, descendant of an old family which had fallen on hard times, was father of a general, an admiral and a

Master of the Rolls: Lord Denning broke my great-grandfather's record as the oldest judge in modern times to sit on the Bench.

The Chief Baron, twice-married, sired twenty-four children ('all legitimate', as he liked to point out), with the result that we had innumerable cousins. His fourth son, Sir Charles Edward Pollock, followed his father to the judicial Bench and was the last of the Barons of the Exchequer. He and I were exactly a hundred years apart (less a few weeks) because he was nearly fifty-one when my father was born, and my father nearly forty-nine when I was born. Baron Pollock never retired, but was taken ill while trying a case and died in 1897 when my father was just twenty-three, down from Cambridge and articled to a relation in a firm of lawyers which rejoiced in the name of Dodgson, Bischoff, Dodgson, Cox and Bumpus.

If the Pollocks brought the brains (though they rather missed my father) my mother's family brought the art. She was a Powell – pronounced to rhyme with *Noel*, as her older cousin Baden-Powell used to point out. (Before founding the Scouts, Baden-Powell had been the hero of the siege of Mafeking, and when London went absurdly wild at the news of the Relief, my mother, then a schoolgirl, was with his family on the balcony, waving to the cheering crowd below.)

Her father, James Crofts Powell, had been a noted designer of stained glass windows. The firm of James Powell of Whitefriars had been designers and makers of glass for three generations, and my grandfather's windows can be found in many churches including the cathedral of St John the Divine in New York. By all accounts he was a delightful man, and his elder son considered that Michael was like him in looks and character; but James Powell had died before any of us were born, and his widow, daughter of a Hampshire and Wiltshire landowner, was the only grandparent I knew.

My mother's side had a sprinkling of admirals, including great-uncle Frank who had brought back from China the four silk scrolls which hung in the hall, part of his loot after helping to suppress the Boxer Rising. Both sides had bishops – long-dead ancestors of my mother, and my father's very alive cousin Bertram, Bishop of Norwich – but the Pollocks had the writers, mostly rather dull and learned.

Perhaps the writer who influenced us most, however, was Lewis Carroll, whose real name was Charles Lutwidge Dodgson. My father's mother, born Amy Dodgson, was Lewis Carroll's first cousin and it was she who brought in the hereditary hardness of hearing. We had aunts, uncles and cousins who were deaf in varying degrees. We talked up to my father, since hearing aids were primitive and little used; the noise at meals must have been deafening as we were inclined to talk all at once at the tops of our voices, except when Daddy came out with a story about stalking, or the law, or the oddities of his relations.

Otherwise, we were hardly yet aware that we had Alice in Wonderland ears.

Besides the affection and security of home we had the good fortune to be sent to one of the happiest and best run preparatory schools of the day, St Peter's, Seaford, on the Sussex coast.

Michael's departure to boarding school was the first break in our companionship, and I recall the end of one holiday when my parents sent us with Nanny to spend the last week in rooms at Seaford. We played happily on the beach and the Downs until the day we must walk up to St Peter's. Michael timed our arrival to coincide with the charabanc (as coaches were called then) which had met the school train. As he greeted old friends, Nanny was delighted to see him go up to a big boy who was teasing a scruffy little junior and sternly tell him to stop.

There was no bullying at St Peter's but the small boy was an oddity, despised and roughed by others; as he wrote to my parents many years later, Michael had taken him under his wing and 'stood by me at a time when I was desperately unhappy. I shall be grateful all my life for his kindness to me in the face of a strong public opinion.'

The minutes flew past. Michael said goodbye and vanished through the boys' entrance. I burst into tears and would not be comforted, either on the walk back or in the lonely parlour of our lodgings, until, in despair, Nanny took me to a toy shop and bought a box of tin soldiers. Mummy was not best pleased when handed a bill for a bribe.

2

The Unspoken Dimension

St Peter's had been built in grounds east of Seaford at the turn of the century, for a grand-daughter of Dr Arnold of Rugby.

Shortly before the 'Great War', as we always called it, a young Scot, R. K. Henderson, bought the school and ran it for twenty years, except for war service in the Grenadier Guards: he nearly always wore a Brigade tie. Tall, with reddish moustache and complexion, he combined a military bearing with a scholarly stoop. He was a good teacher and administrator, if a little skimpy with the food, and devoted to cricket. By the time the Pollock boys began their fourteen years of continuous membership, one after another, he had been joined by Pat Knox-Shaw, who had won the Military Cross but was not military in manner.

Pat was liked and admired by all. He treated us as equals, had no guile or self-importance yet seemed to know everything; his conversation at meals and his teaching were delightful. With Pat's wife and a motherly, old-fashioned matron called Miss Falwaser, and a well-chosen staff, 'R.K.H.' and P.K-S.' ran a school which all three of us enjoyed.

Michael was not outstanding at work or games but he revelled in cricket, which bored me, a duck in a family of devotees – my game was rugger. He loved music and acting. Pat Knox-Shaw, who became headmaster after Henderson's retirement, recalled him long afterwards as ' . . . obviously good within and possessing great charm. He seemed content with his own thoughts and did not obtrude them on others or play to the gallery. But put him on the stage and one realised at once that there was much more imagination and fire than he ever allowed to come to the surface.'

In 1932 I joined him at St Peter's, and according to the custom with brothers we were put next to each other in the same dormitory despite the gap in age. After lights-out we used to run through *The Mikado* or *The Yeoman of the Guard*, *sotto voce*, a little each night. We did more. 'John and I are writing a comic opera,' Michael wrote home on 26 February 1933, in his only letter to survive from St Peter's. 'It is called "Helgardo" and we propose to act it on the stage when we've made it. I am going to write another afterwards, if I can.' The opera disappeared without trace.

In the autumn of 1933 he went on to Charterhouse; we wrote to each other regularly and tried to write a play. Michael became an enthusiastic Carthusian, creeping slowly up the school in work and games, since his performance never equalled the enjoyment he had from history and literature, cricket and music. Only in acting was he outstanding. His friendship with Ian Wallace grew out of their shared interest in theatricals: ' . . . but Michael and I soon realised that while we were both perfectly happy in our different Houses at school, and got on well with our confreres, not all of them found the same things amusing. We both had a highly developed sense of the ridiculous in others – and in ourselves. It was a delight to express an opinion and watch Michael's slow smile of pleasure at being able to agree.'

Their being kindred spirits 'was important to Michael because he was shy', reflected Ian as he recalled their friendship: 'He also had an unaffected dignity, which was inborn and sprang from honesty and integrity, qualities which were second nature to him. I remember him light hearted, and shaking with silent laughter when something amused him. He wasn't unsophisticated, yet every now and then his discovery of something might be delayed a little – perhaps because of his deafness. On these occasions his expression of wonderment at the ways of the world was very engaging.' The slight deafness was not yet apparent to casual acquaintances, nor did it spoil his music. In a later generation he would have been fitted with an invisible hearing aid but the clumsy contraptions of his day were considered a last resort.

Michael and I continued to enjoy school, apart from the usual glooms or worries of a schoolboy, but the holidays were the peaks of the year. Each of us had friends of our own age (three of my four closest friends at St Peter's were to be killed in the war) and sometimes Michael was busy with Martin or Honor on matters too old for me, but our happiest times were together.

In winter we were invited to many shows and films (Michael had a rich godfather) and my mother took us to concerts and introduced us to opera. We always found something to do, for television was not yet on the market to stifle enterprise. We went for

long walks in the West End; we loved second-hand
bookshops; we pored over current affairs and with
Martin invented a mythical country and held debates
or wrote its history; and we produced 'Pollock Brothers'
shows for friends and relations to mark our parents'
anniversaries.

The highlights of spring were country visits, especially to elderly Aunt Joa (Daddy's half-sister) who lived
with another dear spinster, 'Aunt' Violet Martineau, at
Park Corner, a roomy old house in the park which
the nation had given to the Great Duke of Wellington
after Waterloo, at Stratfield Saye in Hampshire.
Following breakfast Aunt Violet read short family
prayers attended by the indoor servants; then Michael
and I spent hours playing wide games in the woods,
which became for us the North West Frontier of
India, right up to the magnificent avenue of Wel-
lingtonias planted in memory of the Great Duke,
who died the year that sequoias were first introduced into England. Back at the house, lunch was
an intellectual as well as a culinary feast, always
ending with 'lunch cake'. Next we would visit the
kitchen to thank Mrs Maynard, the cook, and then
explore the garden or call at the lodges; Michael
was a favourite with the cook and the gardener,
the cowman and old Grove, the chauffeur, and their
families.

On a wet day we had the run of the aunts' libraries
which included all the volumes of *Punch*, a window
into the social and political history of England since
1841. And in the evening there might be charades,
with Aunt Violet as Queen Victoria and Michael as the
Kaiser.

Back in London Michael spent many hours at cricket,

joining Surrey County's schoolboy practice nets and watching the matches. 'I hope John didn't mind me going to the Oval nearly every day for the last week or so but since I didn't get much practice I wanted to make up for it.' He never reached the school's 1st Eleven.

The summer holidays were the best, for my parents always took a house in the country, our favourite being at Croughton near the borders of Oxfordshire, Buckinghamshire and Northamptonshire, where we went for five summers. The owner was a lady-in-waiting to the Duchess of York and thus, after 1936, to the Queen, and would go to Balmoral leaving the house without anything locked up, and the use of gardener, chauffeur and groom, who taught me to ride while Michael had his fill of schoolboy cricket matches at the country houses nearby. We played tennis, boated on the tiny lake, swam at Stowe, and bicycled miles on almost empty lanes. Before breakfast we would rush about with Simon, the cairn terrier, and the two house dogs, chasing rabbits in the small walled park beside the common which afterwards became an American airbase.

By the Coronation summer of 1937 Michael, rising eighteen, was growing fairly tall. He was slender and good-looking, with the step of an athlete. His head-master, Robert Birley, thought him 'an extraordinarily delightful boy. Simple and modest and at the same time with a real grace of manner, which is the only expression I can think of to describe it'; and his cousin and contemporary, Hugh Powell, one of his best friends, remembered that once when they went to a Marx Brothers farce 'Michael laughed so much the management asked us to leave!'

Michael was a good companion rather than a leader. He gave no sign that he was likely to step out of the mould of his circle.

One subject was never discussed between us, except casually; yet religion was the unspoken dimension, taken for granted as part of life's background.

My mother had read to us from Bible story books and then from the Bible until we could read it ourselves, and had taught us to say our prayers. The church we attended had a crowded children's service, and to read the lesson, balancing on a couple of hassocks, was as memorable as the church bazaar or the nativity play.

In term-time St Peter's marched down to Seaford parish church each Sunday morning, joining boys and girls of all the other thirty-six schools, except for Roman Catholic Ladymead; and on Sunday evening we had shortened Evensong in The Hut, an old army hut which served as gymnasium, lecture hall, indoor playground, and as a chapel until the school built its own, after our time. Pat Knox-Shaw and his second master, Basil Talbot, read the age-old prayers of the liturgy in a simple, direct way which sank them deep into our minds.

A Christian outlook was the foundation of my parents' characters. They lived, as it were, by Psalm 15: 'Lord, who shall dwell in thy tabernacle or who shall rest upon thy holy hill? Even he that leadeth an uncorrupt life and doeth the thing which is right, and speaketh the truth from his heart . . .' When Good Friday was ordered to be a working day during the war, my father spluttered into his toast and marmalade: 'It goes against my faith to work on Good Friday!' Yet personal religion was too private to discuss: they were typical of thousands of inarticulate Anglicans in an age when the Evangelical Revival and the Oxford Movement had imperceptibly coalesced to make England what it was between the wars: a land where the yardstick of manners and morals was Christianity, whether personally rejected, ignored or practised.

This was never more evident than in Holy Week and at Easter. Good Friday was respected even by those who did not go to church: a quiet seemed to descend on the land. 'I like best of all,' I wrote in 1937, 'the Good Fridays and Easters I have spent at Park Corner. Lovely services at Stratfield Saye, a quiet ramble with Michael after, and then there is always the charming hospitality of Aunts Joa and Violet.'

That year of 1937 Easter fell early, before St Peter's had broken up for the holidays. The parish church held a special Good Friday service for schools. The parson conducted it from the pulpit in cassock only, the cross and candlesticks were heavily veiled and we sang the sombre hymns of the Passion. I remember having 'a strange feeling of gloom and longing for it all to be over'.

Easter Day was a contrast, not merely because chocolate eggs replaced hot cross buns. 'That is only the "presents" side of it,' I wrote that evening. 'I have a feeling of happiness which is indescribable. The church looked lovely in white, with lots of flowers, and the Easter hymns and anthems are so nice. I can't get some of the tunes out of my head. The Hallelujah Chorus was played too at the end.'

Michael might have felt the same but neither he nor I was aware of a vital missing factor in our lives. However, my closest friend at St Peter's was a boy called Peter Acworth who went on to the Naval College at Dartmouth and, all too soon, would be killed in action at sea. His father was a retired naval captain who was naval correspondent of the *Daily Telegraph* and, as I learned long after, a devoted, humble Christian. Peter's character convinces me in retrospect that he too was a Christian in a way which neither Michael nor I had discovered.

I suspect that Peter prayed for me. If so, he was a link in all that was to happen.

3

Such a Lovable Person

On 24 May 1938 the huge War Memorial chapel at Charterhouse, a tall, long building of distinctive design, a landmark on the ridge above Godalming in Surrey, was the scene of a great service to celebrate the two hundredth anniversary of the conversion of John Wesley, one of the most famous of all Old Carthusians: in his day Charterhouse had been in London.

The only boys to be present were the members of the school choir, including Michael among the tenors and myself, now in the third quarter (term) of my first year, among the trebles. The congregation were seated early, and when we walked in we met the visual impact of massed pews of middle-aged Methodists from all over the country, facing each other across our central aisle.

They hardly needed the school choir: their great Methodist hymns echoed from the high roof. Then Robert Birley, the young headmaster, not yet thirty-five years old, the tall, red-headed historian who would become one of the most important figures in British education in the mid-twentieth century, rose in his stall at the far west end of the chapel to read from

the famous entry in John Wesley's Journal for 24 May
1738. Birley was interested in Wesley (and in John
Newton) and had discovered among old uncatalogued
books in the school library an early eighteenth-century
text book with *John Westley* on the fly leaf. He was
also a good reader, never spoiling a passage by over
emphasis.

'In the evening,' he read, 'I went very unwillingly to
a society in Aldersgate Street, where one was reading
Luther's preface to the Epistle to the Romans. About
a quarter before nine, while he was describing the
change which God works in the heart through faith
in Christ, I felt my heart strangely warmed. I felt I
did trust in Christ, Christ alone for salvation; and
an assurance was given me that he had taken away
my sins, even *mine*, and saved *me* from the law of sin
and death.'

As I listened, my heart too was 'strangely warmed'.
John Wesley seemed to be talking about a Christianity
which had escaped me. But no one explained what
Wesley meant, and the strange warming cooled.

Michael made no comment on the service in my
hearing. We did not talk much together at school,
since a boy in his first year must not consort with a
house monitor, even if they were brothers. However,
we shared a sleeping cubicle, so that after the clanging
of the waking bell before early school I would fetch
his cup of the hot liquid which they called coffee. I
also had the run of his tiny study as well as that
of the fagmaster he had chosen for me from his
friends.

That summer of 1938 would be the end of Michael's
education. My father could not afford to send all his
three sons to Cambridge: Martin had gone to Trinity

as the eldest, had taken his degree and was completing his articles in the office of a London solicitor. I was expected to win a Trinity scholarship in history, which would help with the fees; thus Michael was left out.

If, however, I was ahead of him, comparatively, in intellect, he was far ahead of me in character, which was well described by the wife of W. C. Sellar, the Charterhouse master who was co-author of the celebrated history skit, *1066 and All That*. The Sellars took parties of older boys to ski in Switzerland and in January 1938 they had invited Michael. Hope Sellar saw him seldom after he left Charterhouse; her description relates to Michael before the great event which redirected his life. 'Such a lovable person,' she wrote. 'So essentially kind and simple and warm hearted.' Michael and I were both interested in people but whereas I tended to be critical Michael saw what was good. His kindness, happy nature and even temper gave him a popularity which he neither sought nor exploited.

Michael had no clear plan for his career, whereas I had mine mapped: after Cambridge I would go to the Bar, the Pollock 'trade'; would become a high court judge like my grandfather, and end up in the House of Lords like Cousin Ernest, late Master of the Rolls! Michael's options were limited. He agreed to go on the Stock Exchange for, if not handy with figures, his way with people might make him a useful stockbroker. My father signed him up with a firm which ran a course in accountancy for intending brokers and jobbers.

The family holiday of 1938 passed all too quickly at Croughton, with a fortnight afterwards in the West

Country for Michael and me and our parents. Then he began his daily grind in the City, coinciding with the Munich Crisis; air raid trenches appeared in the squares and parks and when I returned to Charterhouse we all spent weary hours digging them in peculiarly hard ground before Chamberlain returned from Hitler with the scrap of paper which promised 'Peace in our time'.

When the promise of peace wore thin, early in 1939, Michael and two Old Carthusian friends in the City, Douglas MacCallan and Gordon Anthony, joined the Inns of Court Officers' Training Corps. They pretended that they joined for the social pleasures of this elite body but every young man wanted to be ready if war broke out, and the Inns of Court could bring a quick commission. The training sessions were a relief from a dreary stockbroking office. The other consolations were the London Season, with debutante dances and dinner parties in white tie and tail coat; and concerts, opera, and opportunities to watch Test or County cricket.

We had one last glorious summer holiday at Croughton under the shadow of war. In mid-August Martin was called up with the Royal Naval Volunteer Reserve and went to sea. Our parents had planned to take Michael and me to join two cousins on the North Cornwall coast but we reached no farther than Oxford when a man held up an evening newspaper – *Poland Invaded* – and we turned back. Next day Michael was ordered to Sandhurst, which had been changed overnight from the professionals' Royal Military College into an Officer Cadet Training Unit for armoured regiments. Michael was not sorry to abandon stockbroking.

We met again a week later at our sister's wedding, hurriedly brought forward so that she could follow the drum with her Territorial officer bridegroom, who soon transferred to the Coldstream Guards. My parents and I moved out of London to Northaw in south Hertfordshire, an easy daily journey for my father to his office near the Law Courts. From there I went back to school.

That autumn began a train of events, momentous for me and later for Michael.

Robert Birley had brought in another young Eton master to be senior chaplain at Charterhouse. George Snow, as tall as Birley, with a deep voice, was son of a general and afterwards became a headmaster and then a suffragan bishop. Unlike many ordained schoolmasters of the time he was zealous, not merely taking services and teaching divinity but aiming to foster the religious and moral life of the boys, both individually (he had a pastoral touch) and in the crowd.

Seizing the opportunity of the national mood he planned an informal Christian Fellowship of boys and masters. A master who joined was Tommy Garnett, the tutor (under-housemaster) of our house, Saunderites, which was one of the original Victorian school buildings on three sides of Founders Court, a lawn looking across to the western playing fields and the open country beyond. T. R. Garnett was then twenty-five, a Cambridge cricket blue and a county player for Somerset. Later, after war service, he became headmaster of Marlborough and then of Geelong in Australia, where Prince Charles was one of his pupils.

Snow hoped that each house would include a small

group of boys who would undertake to pray privately each morning and meet weekly to increase their understanding of Christianity, strengthen their characters and improve the tone of their house. In Saunderites he and Garnett selected as leader a boy a year older than myself. Derek asked me to help him as he knew that I read the Bible. He and I collected a few other boys and in the first weeks of winter we met at the invitation of our elderly matron, Miss Jennings, an archdeacon's daughter. On Sunday evenings we went to Tommy Garnett's room where he read from religious books or the Bible to any who cared to join us.

Derek came from the Lake District. Athletic and strong, a fair scholar and a forceful personality with plenty of humour, he would be killed by a shell in Germany in the last weeks of the war, directing his platoon's fire to break up a counter-attack. Derek soon became my closest schoolfriend, and when we returned from the Christmas holidays, which I had much enjoyed because Michael had been given generous leave from Sandhurst, we shared a study. The weather of January 1940 was bitter but Robert Birley himself had taken over Saunderites, and the diet and conditions improved despite the war. Our little discussion group resumed. Derek and I bossed it; but we had little idea how to make our surroundings 'more Christian'.

I thought that anyone who said his or her prayers, read the Bible and tried to follow Christ's teaching and example was a good Christian; and that everyone in Britain except those of Jewish faith was some sort of Christian (Hindu and Muslim minorities had not yet come) and that we struggled up the hill by different routes. By trying hard I might please God enough to be granted His presence in a special way and to understand

the Bible better, though parts did not concern me, or
were outdated; Derek and I judged the Bible by our own
tastes and by the little we knew of biblical scholarship
at third or fourth hand.

Jesus Christ did not fit easily into our picture except
as a moral teacher and the supreme example of love and
patience: the crucifixion was a mystery, the resurrection
a distant event which we accepted as part of the historic
faith, and the Holy Spirit did not fit anywhere. We were
much too grown-up to speak of Christ as a 'Friend' or
as 'the Lord Jesus', like little children. Older people
prayed to the Father. I never felt close to the Father,
nor knew of answered prayer; yet I was sure He must
be pleased with our efforts, although I labelled myself
a sinner when I remembered.

One of our number, however, spoke in the most
natural way of 'the Lord Jesus', to our thinly disguised
amusement. Richard, whose brother Tom had been
Michael's exact contemporary in Saunderites and had
gone into the Regular Army, was quiet and small and
wanted to be a farmer: he won a First at Cambridge
and afterwards farmed in Norfolk. He was the only one
of us whose character could be described as Christian,
yet we despised him because he would not argue; he
simply let us know that the first step in being Christian
was to become one – by receiving 'the Lord Jesus' into
your life through a definite act of faith. Only then
would Derek and I be able to live for our best Friend,
who would never leave us nor forsake us.

4

On the Precipice

Every Sunday afternoon Richard used to go to the school Christian Union which, in 1940, though officially recognised as a school society, was not much encouraged by the chaplains. The CU met in a small room in the basement of a private house on Charterhouse Hill for a short talk by a visiting speaker. He was generally an officer of 'Camp', a holiday houseparty of boys from many public schools, sponsored by the Scripture Union. I had once attended a few of the CU meetings, in too critical a spirit to benefit.

Boys of the Christian Union lived out their faith but did not parade it; if asked, they made plain that it did not derive from their own cleverness or goodness but from the presence of the living Christ in their hearts. That, though such adjectives could never be pinned on Richard, sounded to me proud, narrow-minded and emotional.

Derek agreed with me – or so I believed, until on the evening of Sunday 4 February 1940 he came into our study, beaming, and astonished me by saying that he had joined the Christian Union. He had been to their meeting that afternoon, and on to tea with the speaker (who had delighted him by quoting Keats as he poured out the tea).

I had not realised that Derek had been growing increasingly unhappy. Unknown to me he had been talking long with the CU leader, whom he knew because they both played football for Charterhouse in the 1st Eleven; the snow had stopped practices and given plenty of time for talk.

Derek told me how he had slowly realised that his efforts at self-improvement fell short of God's demands; that he knew nothing of God, and that whenever he tried to reach him, sin blocked the way. Then the other boy had showed him the verse from Isaiah 53: 'All we like sheep have gone astray; we have turned every one to his own way; and the Lord hath laid on him the iniquity of us all.'

That very morning he had made that verse his own, by asking Christ into his life as Saviour and Master; and, said Derek in his vigorous way, his new joy, peace and assurance, as well as God's promises in the Bible, had convinced him that now, and not before, he was a true Christian. I retorted that talk of receiving Christ once for all was rot. We talked that evening and the next, for school work in the History VIth was undemanding because a flu epidemic had disrupted all schedules.

I discussed the question intellectually: 'Would this help my ability to become a true Christian?' As I weighed the pros and cons, I remained unimpressed by the thought that if sin mattered in the way Derek urged, then I needed Christ, and until I had found Him, I was not a Christian. Yet I could not ignore Derek's new, warm experience which made more sense and difference to him every day; and he did not let matters rest. His burden to me was: 'You *need* Him.'

Then Richard showed me an American booklet which shook me, because *The Victorious Life* was so different from mine. Derek and Richard must have been praying. Moreover, a strong feeling was invading me that I must abandon my proud plans for a legal career, and serve God in His Church; if possible, the overseas Church; and I was not worthy.

On Ash Wednesday, 7 February the entire question shifted: Derek was right, I *needed* Christ.

In whatever corner of my soul I looked, sin was contaminating and spoiling. The real Christian life was above my hardest efforts. My arguments went by the board as I saw that sin did not mean only words and deeds which a man of honour would spurn as mean or ungentlemanly or indecent. Sin lay in the small matters too; the peevishness and intolerance, the petty selfishness, the unkind word, the impure thought, things that 'everyone did' which had never previously worried me.

Above all, it lay in the pride which condemned others and condoned self, which grew with every attempt at self-reform, and sought to pile up merit before God while refusing to yield to His love and claims. I saw myself guilty, and my good deeds as 'filthy rags' in God's sight; and I was powerless to fight my way out.

I had thought that if I made myself good enough for Him, Christ would come to me. I had got it the wrong way round. The unselfishness, happiness and peace of mind which I admired in Richard and now – rather strikingly – in Derek, was not the *cause* of their knowing Christ but the result; and now I wanted Him, too.

One Bible verse in particular nagged at me, which later I discovered had led Charles Wesley to conversion in 1783: Galatians 2:20: 'I am crucified with Christ: nevertheless I live; yet not I, but Christ liveth in me: and the life which I now live in the flesh I live by the faith of the Son of God, who loved me, and gave himself for me.' Christ did not live in me; I longed for Him, and I knew that life would be hopeless until I found Him.

Out of school hours I would walk by myself in the frozen grounds, and in the woods above the River Wye. I made use of the newly opened small Founder's Chapel, formed from the chancel of the old chapel, where the nave was being redesigned as a music school and concert hall; and the more I struggled and prayed, the more miserable I became.

I knew that Christ had died for me and I now knew His promise in Revelation 3: 20: 'Behold, I stand at the door, and knock: if any man hear my voice, and open the door, I will come in.' The Risen Christ, 'who loved me', was waiting to enter by His Holy Spirit and I was pleading 'Come in'; but my hand lay hard on the latch, barring His entry.

His coming would mean relief and joy and peace, but I could not bring myself to ask Him in by a simple prayer and then step out in faith, feelings or no feelings, relying solely on His promise. I looked for emotion – and got nothing. I would willingly have tried some great labour to cleanse my sin, but not this simple step, dropping every effort.

The days wore on, and I was dissatisfied and useless. I tried to work up faith – once I thought I had found Christ, after spending fifty minutes alone in Founder's Chapel. While light snow fell outside I worked up wonderful feelings, but the next morning I was back in desolation.

Both Birley and his wife were down with flu, and also the matron and the headmonitor, and many boys; others had German measles. Michael and Martin, on leave together, had flu at Northaw. My own slight bout had been earlier; my present sickness was spiritual.

I was desperate, yet I would not take that one step into the unknown. It seemed as if I stood on the edge of a cliff with no way back. Between me and the promised land of peace and happiness and service lay a chasm. I must step off into the darkness, trusting in the unseen hand of Christ to catch me and land me safe on the other side; the whole of life had to be placed unreservedly in His hands, or nothing at all, and I could not bring myself to let go.

On the second Thursday, 15 February 1940, I was utterly despondent all morning and afternoon, feeling far from Christ. After tea, as we sat in our study, Derek suggested that we pray together. He had wisely not pressed me but now sensed that the moment had come. He referred again, gently, to Christ on the cross: how He had so loved the world that He had given Himself to die; how the sinner's guilt had been laid on Him, the Redeemer and Saviour. Derek reminded me of Christ's words in that verse in Revelation: 'Behold, I stand at the door and knock . . .' Derek suggested that I open the door and ask the Lord Jesus in, praying aloud.

I had never prayed aloud extempore, but now we bowed our heads and shut our eyes. Strength was gone; I could struggle no more. I simply told the Lord Jesus, aloud, that I wanted to be forgiven. I told Him that I believed He had died for me and had promised to 'come in'. I asked Him in. There was no emotion, none

of the splendid feelings I had sought, but this time I said
to myself, 'He must be in my heart – I have claimed His
promise and He cannot break it.'

A few moments later a boy walked in whom I disliked
for no good reason; after the war this Saunderite not
only rose to the very top of his profession but was also
much loved by all who worked with him. Without any
conscious effort the thought came at once: I must not
dislike him, for the Lord Jesus lives in me now, who
loves him.

Soon I had to go to choir practice in the old music
schools, knowing that whether or not I felt him, 'Christ
lives in me'. One hour later, quite unlooked for and
unexpected, as I walked back in the starlight, with the
snow underfoot, the most wonderful sense of joy and
forgiveness filled my soul. The burden and the misery
had gone. In their place were peace and spontaneous
praise; I spoke to the Lord Jesus as a Friend and
experienced something of the joy and freedom He
promised. That very night the Bible became a new
book to me, a message from my new Friend, teaching
and encouraging me and revealing Himself.

A housemaster was giving a series of lectures to the
upper school on musical appreciation, illustrated by
gramophone records. That Friday, his subject was
Tchaikovsky's Fifth Symphony. When he played the
main theme in the minor key of the earlier movements
it seemed to echo my gloomy search, so recently ended,
for spiritual light. Then he put on the entire final
movement in which the theme emerges triumphantly
in the major key until the end. In tune with the music I
opened my heart yet wider to Christ, with overwhelm-
ing joy. A few days later at a gramophone concert the
entire Fifth Symphony thrilled me as a commentary on

the past two weeks. Many years afterwards, visiting Soviet Christians in Central Asia at the height of the Khrushchev repression of religion, I was able to tell them how their great composer had helped to confirm my conversion.

Each day now was a joy, despite inevitable temporary doubts, and perhaps too much bubbling of the new wine. Derek, Richard and I, of the original group, were growing together, helped by the Christian Union. On my second Sunday the speaker was Eric Nash, the quiet clergyman always known as 'Bash', who had founded Camp eleven years before. His balanced leadership and pithy talks, letters and advice brought scores of public schoolboys into lifelong Christian ministry, while his diplomacy dispersed the prejudices of headmasters and chaplains.

I had never heard Christian truth put so simply and clearly as in Bash's talk in the basement room on Charterhouse Hill that Sunday. He spoke, as I wrote in my daily diary (which did not last the year), about 'how we must open every "room" in our minds to the Lord Jesus; and when I reflected I found that I had not done so. There were still one or two rooms where He was not. I had a short chat with Bash afterwards and Derek stayed on and spoke for an hour with him.'

Back at Saunderites I attended the Sunday evening Bible Reading in the house tutor's room. 'And it was then,' I wrote in my diary, 'and not until then, I know, that I opened every door to the Lord Jesus. Then there descended on me such a quiet certainty, joy and peace of mind that I have never had before. Ten days ago I opened the "Front Door". Now every door is open, I feel sure.'

Another Saunderite in our original group, Hugh,

'opened the door' that Sunday as Bash spoke; and next month Hugh and I, with two other boys and one master, were confirmed by the Bishop of Guildford in his private chapel at Farnham Castle. We had been prepared by Snow and our former housemaster, and Snow brought the Confirmation forward rather than our waiting until a large number were confirmed in the summer.

Bishop Macmillan understood boys: his address was apt; the service most moving, especially as Derek, who was already confirmed, had been invited. And when we moved into the Episcopal dining-room we found that while our grown-ups stood around nibbling thin bread and butter, we boys sat down to a table groaning with buns, sandwiches and every kind of cake.

5

Dunkirk Summer

I did not tell Michael about my great change.

Michael was enjoying Sandhurst with his two Old Carthusian friends from the Inns of Court, Gordon Anthony and Douglas MacCallan. The Phoney War seemed remote. Their plentiful leave included weekly half-holidays and most weekends, and London parties were easily reached. The other two pretended to be jealous, recalled Gordon, 'that Michael always managed to get invited to a function by a deb – more so than we did. It must have been his good looks. We used to joke with Michael that he must be the one and only who had gone through a whole Season without it costing him a brass cent.' 'He enjoyed dances,' remembered Douglas, 'but was always slightly reserved, or in control of himself. He had no flamboyance but plenty of charm.'

The three friends got into the usual scrapes, though Michael kept out of the others' plot to secrete sandwiches and beer to refresh themselves on sentry duty – which, if discovered, would have brought expulsion. Once Gordon, when in charge of the squad, courteously gave the 'Eyes Right' to salute a cadet's fiancée but the Regimental Sergeant Major happened to be looking and put him under close arrest. He was sentenced to four Saturday drills, and 'Michael and Douglas continued to hit bright London without me.'

By spring 1940 their commissions were in sight. The adjutant of the Inns of Court had been asked by the crack cavalry regiments in the Royal Armoured Corps to look out for suitable officers, and he put up the three Carthusians for the Queen's Bays (2nd Dragoon Guards): with the Foot Guards and the Household Cavalry, these were traditionally regarded as the elite of the British Army, though the place of honour on parade is always given to the guns, and thus to the men serving them.

All the older officers of the Bays were skilled horsemen, whereas Michael had not been interested in riding; but after mechanisation they wanted young men of good background and personality, with natural gifts of leadership rather than mere military skills, provided these were present. Michael, however, might have failed some of the passing out examination had not the Commandant of Sandhurst, an old friend of Daddy's, gone out of his way to arrange extra tuition.

During the Easter holidays Michael and I were only together one day. My spiritual discovery seemed too intimate to describe to a brother who was also my dearest friend; I longed that he should know the Lord Jesus, yet I could do nothing but pray.

On the day the Phoney War ended, as Denmark fell and Norway began her bitter, doomed resistance, I went down to Iwerne Minster in Dorset for my first Camp, or holiday houseparty, which met for the first time in the spacious, elegant Victorian mansion of Jacobean style, built for Lord Wolverton in 1878 by Waterhouse and bought in 1933 by Clayesmore School. Camp had rented south coast preparatory schools until the outbreak of war, but Clayesmore proved so suitable that it became the permanent site.

'Everybody seems awfully nice,' I noted, 'and it is easy to get to know people as everybody seems out to get to know everyone else.' I found 'ragger' (rugger and soccer football mixed informally) and hockey great fun, a proof indeed of my conversion, for a few months earlier I would have loathed the thought of spending part of the holidays playing organised or disorganised games with other schoolboys. At prayers in the evening, Bash spoke on the Parable of the Treasure hidden in the Field, which began a series of outstanding talks by officers who included Maurice Wood, a future D-Day hero when a chaplain, and later Bishop of Norwich. John Stott, the future theologian and evangelist, then head boy of Rugby, was Camp secretary.

That first Camp strengthened my faith and opened vistas of discipleship and service. Back at school, the spring and summer of 1940 were the happiest I had ever known, despite the unbelievable French collapse and the sound of gunfire from France, audible even to us, deep in Surrey. I was able to bring an Austrian boy in my house to trust in Christ; his world had collapsed at the Anschluss of 1938 and he had grown blacker in mind and looks as each German victory made invasion of England more probable. The change when Otto trusted Christ was noticeable and I proudly presented him when Bash came to the Christian Union, now meeting in a pleasant Georgian drawing room, on 26 May, the Sunday before Dunkirk.

The day previous Michael had passed out of Sand-hurst, with Douglas and Gordon, and they became second lieutenants in the Queen's Bays. The Regiment was contesting the crossing of the Somme, thus drawing off German troops from Dunkirk, and then making a fighting retreat across north-western France. Three new young officers could not be of use at that late stage of the campaign and they were ordered to the armoured training school at Bovington in Dorset.

As the Dunkirk evacuation began, and the little boats rushed to the rescue, I went down with a bad attack of measles and spent Britain's 'Finest Hour' ignominiously in the sanatorium, emerging on the day Paris fell. By then, Charterhouse was in the grip of invasion fever, digging a tank trap (in a marsh) and practising defence, fitting out air raid shelters and watching an aerial dog fight above our heads. We were all very determined, with unshakeable faith in ultimate victory, but in recording my decision to go to the school farming camp and then to Iwerne, which would also be a farming camp, I added: 'But of course, the Lord Jesus may work it out differently. After all, Hitler says he will be in London on 15th August, and every date he has given so far has been proved correct. But we are safe in the Lord Jesus.'

And not only safe; the unfolding, deepening friendship, wholly undeserved, with 'Jesu, joy of man's desiring' gave an inner beauty to those summer days of distant conflict; and the Bible, which I had supposed I knew well, proved to be unexplored territory with exciting discoveries, whether alone in a brief morning or evening quiet time, or together with the others. Nor were opportunities lacking to show our faith by our works; when the house domestic staff dispersed to the war we took on the chores, pending a new system, with such gusto that the house tutor rightly rebuked us for growing a trifle smug and exclusive.

When the summer holidays came, I and another boy (later killed in action in the RAF) bicycled from Hertfordshire all the way down to George Snow's camp on his cousin's estate at Forde Abbey in Dorset, thus giving me a lasting memory of the quiet roads and scenery of southern England before the great post-war smothering by vehicles and buildings. We had a back-breaking fortnight: we pulled weeds, stooked corn and thinned plantations at Forde Abbey, while the Battle of Britain raged farther east; at the camp fire each evening, George Snow conducted a sweepstake, before the nine o'clock news, on the number of enemy aircraft shot down.

Derek and I then bicycled on to Iwerne, where the traditional and spiritual life of Camp was cleverly dovetailed into the demands of wartime farming and forestry.

At Camp I thought and prayed frequently about Michael, who was with his Regiment under canvas near Warminster on the northern edge of Salisbury Plain: after the Fall of France, the Bays had been among the last British troops to leave the Continent. They were now part of the strategic reserve against the expected invasion. A new commanding officer had taken over soon after the three Old Carthusians joined. Lieutenant-Colonel G. W. C. ('Tom') Draffen was a fine horseman and athlete and already experienced in command. He was short in stature, very even-tempered and unflappable, with a twinkle in his eyes. Nearly thirty years later he wrote: 'I remember thinking how lucky we were to have three such nice boys. Commanding officers and indeed anyone in authority should not have favourites, or certainly should not show it, but I confess among the subalterns of that time, Michael was one of my favourites. He was keen, well-mannered

– and always cheerful, a great asset, especially in wartime.'

Michael was delighted to be an officer in the Bays. His attitude was well expressed by another young officer of 1940, Michael Halsted, who felt in retrospect that both of them 'admired the independent but closely knit cavalry spirit, and were excited and honoured to be admitted to a brotherhood of brave tradition whose strength lay, among other qualities, in supreme self-confidence, and refusal to be bogged down by narrow or petty outlook or action. Our officers were the most tolerant of men, the most liberal and open minded; and the most concerned for their men.' They were a family rather than a unit; the Bays, like my own future Regiment, the Coldstream Guards, took hazards in their stride and rose above discomfort or suffering, whether in action or training.

Michael was given Number One Troop, 'A' Squadron. He was thus in command of eleven men and three very expensive tanks. An armoured regiment had three squadrons of four troops each, together with a larger headquarters squadron. The Bays totalled about 450 men (not counting those away on staff or detached duties) including about forty officers. Each squadron had seven officers.

The Troop Sergeant of 1 Troop was Ronnie Strutt, who would win the Military Medal in Tunisia as a squadron sergeant-major, become Regimental Sergeant Major in Italy and later be commissioned in the Regiment, retiring as a major. He recalled Michael's taking over: 'He did not have to play himself in. On the first meeting one could see the kind of man he was. We all liked and respected him.' Most of his troopers were not regulars but volunteers or conscripts from varied occupations. Like citizen soldiers everywhere, they would play up young subalterns if they could. On the whole they did not find Michael easy to deceive, but he had a habit of ingenuously cupping his hand to an ear if he did not quite hear, and they soon discovered that they could say what they shouldn't when out of his range!

Before leaving Camp that summer I asked Bash's advice: How could I win Michael for Christ? Bash replied: 'Be like a dentist. You know how they probe around before doing anything. Put out a feeler, see if he is ready.'

Michael and I had been writing to each other fairly often. A letter, therefore, was the obvious probe. I was too busy at Camp, and the Blitz too noisy at Northaw, where my parents and I went out each evening in our tin helmets to watch London Docks burning, away to the south, until the welcome arrival of anti-aircraft guns brought danger from shell-splinters, since Churchill not only put guns in the London parks but also ringed the suburbs and nearby countryside: we had batteries quite close.

Back at Charterhouse, a little farther from the Blitz, I wrote to Michael, proposing a fresh subject for discussion: 'What does it mean to be a true Christian?'

Michael's reply was predictable: to be a Christian meant being decent, kind, going to church etc., and his own object in life was to go out of his way to help people – which it was; moreover, Michael usually said his prayers and was never much of a swearer. An occasional 'Damn!' exhausted his repertoire. Then Michael sprang a delightful surprise. He looked forward, he wrote, to hearing my views in person, for the Regiment would move to Surrey very shortly, and his Squadron's winter quarters would be at Tilford, only five miles from Charterhouse.

I knew that I must write again at once, for I could put in a letter what would be hard to tell him face to face. On the evening of 4 October 1940, five days before my seventeenth birthday, I settled down in my little study. The air raid siren wailed, distant thuds came from the London Blitz, and at one point the lights failed and I continued for a time by candle. The letter filled eleven close-packed sides.

I posted it next morning and he received it the following day, 6 October, at Longbridge Deverill on Salisbury Plain. Noticing that I had written many pages, he waited until he was off duty and carried the letter to his tent, after dinner in the Officers' Mess tent. As he started to read, Michael was immediately interested because instead of the debating tone he had expected, this second letter had almost too intense an earnestness. After a few paragraphs he realised that whatever I had got, he wanted too.

The letter of a boy just turning seventeen, written off-the-cuff to his brother and best friend, has its limitations. Yet reading it again after fifty years I can see why it hit Michael between the eyes, since until then I had told him nothing of the new turn I had taken.

The first essential was to shatter his assumption, to which our generation had been bred, that trying your best and being helpful made you good enough for God; and thus to shatter his casual hope of working his way to heaven . . .

6

The Letter

'*Dear Michael*,' I wrote: 'Thank you ever so much for your letter and for your remarks on the Christian life. You were very frank, and I will be frank in return. Only I am not going to give you just my opinion – I am going to give you the Bible's opinion (which is, indeed, synonymous with mine).

'We have both been brought up to believe in the Bible, so there is no need to emphasise that it is the Word of God – it is *true*. When you were a history specialist you learnt that every good historian always gives his authorities when making a statement. I am going to do likewise. I should be very pleased if you would look up every reference which I give, so that you may see the truth in black and white. In what follows in this letter you may find remarks which you consider untrue, overbearing or even conceited. All I ask you to remember is that I am speaking in all humility and seriousness, for this is not a question to be trifled with. I am speaking in love, to God and to you. And I am speaking from *personal experience*. Any remark I make will be on the authority of the Bible, and I ask you to read this letter with an entirely open mind.

'First let me give you a frank, straightforward statement: in the opinion of the Bible (and so in my opinion) a Christian is any man, woman or child who comes to God as a lost sinner, accepts the Lord Jesus Christ as their personal Saviour, surrenders to Him as their Lord and Master, confesses Him as such before the world and strives to please Him in everything day by day.

'Now that is a pretty terrific statement, and you may say that "Surely that is not the only way of becoming a Christian? I am doing my best to be good and help others; shall I not go to heaven too?" The answer is, I am afraid, most emphatically "*No*". Let me tell a story: a man was in a barber's chair, and was desirous of telling the barber of salvation. But the barber just said, "I do my best; what more can I do?" The Christian relapsed into silence, until his shave was over and the next customer came in. Then he spoke: "May I shave this customer for you?" he said.

'"No," replied the barber, with a wry smile.

'"But I should do my best," said the Christian.

'"Ah, but your best would not be good enough for this gentleman."

'"Nor," replied the Christian, "is *your* best good enough for God."

'You are asking, "Why is not my best good enough for God?" The answer, hard as it is, is that *You are too great a sinner*. We are all too great sinners for God before we accept Jesus Christ. "But," you reply, "I am popular and never do anyone wrong. I love and am loved." Just think a moment; have you kept the first and greatest commandment all your life? "Thou shalt love the Lord thy God with *all* thy heart and with *all* thy soul and with *all* thy mind" (Matthew 22: 37). Have you kept the commandment given in

1 Corinthians 10: 31, "Whatsoever ye do, do *all* to the glory of God"? There are many other commandments which I could quote, and which both you and I and everyone have broken countless times. Now that is only one side of the question: what about our good deeds? Well, there I had the greatest shock of all, when I was led to Christ. And there too you will receive a shock. In Isaiah 64: 6, we read, "And all our righteousnesses are as *filthy rags*." Again, James 2: 10, "Whosoever shall keep the whole law, and yet offend in one point, he is guilty of *all*." Again, "Except your righteousness shall exceed the righteousness of the Scribes and Pharisees, *ye shall in no case enter into the Kingdom of heaven*" (Matthew 5: 20).

'When all this was put to me I said, "But I have lived sixteen years and everything has gone all right. I have said prayers night and morning and read the Bible, shall I not go to heaven?" I discovered that the answer was *No*. "The wages of sin is *death*; but the *gift* of God is eternal life through Jesus Christ our Lord" (Romans 6: 23). I realised that I was a sinner, I realised that the "whole world lieth in wickedness" (1 John 5: 19), but I thought that there must be some way out for sinners. Think of the countless millions in England alone who have not received the Christ. Are they to die (ie, be separated from God in the life to come)? Yes, unless they accept the Christ.

'Again and again throughout the Bible we are shown that we are wicked and worthy of death. There is no denying it. "The heart is deceitful above all things, and desperately wicked" (Jeremiah 17: 9). "He that believeth not is condemned already" (John 3: 18).

'Just think of all that; it is pretty shattering, isn't it? But, praise be to God, there is a way out. And not only a way out, but a way that leads to *Peace, Joy* and *Eternal Life*.

'And it is so *simple* that thousands just don't believe it.

' "Except a man be born again, he cannot see the kingdom of God" (John 3: 3). The natural man is naturally blind to spiritual truths, and he cannot, however gifted he may be, obey, understand or please God (Romans 8: 7–8). But once we are born again by accepting Jesus into our lives, we can "enter into the kingdom of God". May I say once more that all this is not theory but real fact and experience, so wonderful that it has to be "tasted" to be really appreciated?

'Let's look at John 3. "Except a man be born again, he cannot see the kingdom of God" (verse 3). Read on, slowly and thoughtfully. "How can these things be?" (verse 9) – *"We speak that we do know"* (verse 11). Moses lifted up the serpent in the wilderness, as you may read in Numbers 21: 5–9. The serpent of brass was a miraculous yet simple cure. Jesus also gives us a miraculous and simple cure. "Whosoever believeth on him should not perish but have everlasting life" (John 3: 15). Why? Because "God so loved the world, that he gave his only begotten Son, that whosoever believeth in him should not perish, but have everlasting life." Again, why? Because *"He* was wounded for our transgressions . . . with *his* stripes *we* are healed" (Isaiah 53: 5). God has made Jesus a curse for us, so that we may live. Jesus died on the cross and bore thereon the sins of the whole world. Read 1 Peter 2: 24; Romans 5: 6–11 and Romans 3: 21–26.

'What, then, must we do to be saved? *Just believe with your heart, first confessing all to Him.* It is no use unless you are prepared to tell him everything. He cannot help

Michael on leave with his parents, Summer 1940.

Officers of "A" Squadron, Tilford, December 1940. From left to right: Gordon Anthony, Michael, Jimmy Dance, Alex Barclay, Peter Glyn, Humphrey Weld, Douglas MacCallan.

Churchill with the Bays, August 1941. The Honey tank might have been Michael's in the Msus battle.

The Colonel-in-Chief's Farewell, 17th September 1941 (detail). Lieut-Colonel "Tom" Draffen on the Queen's right; Michael at her left shoulder.

4/
Dont bother to return it. If you want more I can send them to you.

How wonderful He is in the amazing ways he gives us such abounding Joy!

My stay at Park Corner was very short but very enjoyable. I took the opportunity of going out into the woods before breakfast & walking with the Lord. Everything was peaceful save the occasional twitter of the birds in the surrounding trees, or the scamper of a rabbit across my path. How wonderful to be alone with Him, & in such peacefulness.

Before I went Aunt V. said to me privately, "I read that book you told me about every day now — with the Bible". She must have meant! I think, the Scripture Union Notes that you recommended. I cannot think of any other 'book' I have given her — save Lewis

Michael writes to John, 19th April 1941 after a weekend leave to Park Corner.

if you hold something back. "If we confess our sins, he is faithful and just to forgive our sins, and cleanse us from all unrighteousness" (1 John 1: 9). Before Jesus can come into your heart you have got to be emptied of your sins, and only He can do that. Are you prepared to confess that? Your joy and peace on earth and your eternal life or damnation depend on it. *"How shall we escape, if we neglect* so great salvation?" Hebrews 2: 3. "He that believeth on the Son hath everlasting life and he that believeth not the Son shall not see life, but the *wrath of God abideth on him*." Believe that Jesus can come right inside you.

'Do not wait; confess *now*. "Seek ye the Lord while he may be found, call ye upon him when he is near" Isaiah 55: 6. "Boast not thyself of tomorrow, for thou knowest not what a day may bring forth." *"Behold, now is the accepted time, now is the day of salvation"* (2 Corinthians 6: 2). I suggest that you get on your knees before God and pray the following prayer (or words like it.)

'"Lord Jesus, I realise that I am a great sinner, as is everyone who has not accepted thee. Lord, I realise that unless I come to thee I cannot be saved. I also have heard thee say: 'Behold, I stand at the door and knock. If *any man* hear my voice, and open the door, I will come in' (Revelation 3: 20). Jesus, I hear thy knock. Cleanse me, Lord. Search me, O God, and know my heart; try me, and know my thoughts, and see if there be any wicked way in me and lead me in the way everlasting (Psalm 139: 23–4). Jesus, come into my heart now. Give me faith, and thy Holy Spirit. I now surrender, Lord in me abide."

'If that prayer is really *meant*, a new nature will be given you, a new heart. I say that truthfully, and with experience. On February 15th, 1940 I prayed like that, and I knew at once that I had been given a new nature. I struggled from February 4th – February 15th, and it was not until I utterly stopped trying, and just said to God, "I give in, and *trust*" that He came. You must be utterly trusting in Him before He can save you. If you are in the least bit proud or confident in yourself, Jesus cannot do anything. "Except ye be converted, and become as little children, ye shall not enter into the kingdom of heaven" (Matthew 18: 3).

'Now when you ask Jesus into your heart it is *unlikely (though possible) that a sudden miraculous change will be felt at once.* But, believe me, if you trust Jesus at His word and believe you are saved you will soon realise it. Joy will come as it has never come before, because God Almighty is your Best Friend.

'You will soon know you are saved because the Bible will at once become real. Verses you never noticed before will meet your eye. "Peace which passeth all understanding" will enter your heart – though doubts may arise at first. Ten days after I was converted, on February 25th, the Holy Ghost came upon me. That was when I admitted Jesus into every room of my soul. The most marvellous peace descended on me then, and has never left me.

'You will also meet with much opposition in the form of temptation. Satan – a very real person – does not bother about you until you come to Jesus, or begin to come. When temptation comes – *Look to Jesus for He will never leave you* (Hebrews 13: 5).

'A few words on other important subjects may help. *Sin.* Your sins have been forgiven (provided you have truly accepted Jesus). Naturally you will still sin; we all do. But we are no longer at enmity with God, and He will always forgive directly we confess. We are not in a state of sin any more (1 John 3: 3).

'*Prayer*. The Christian life centres round a close friendship with Jesus. This is gained by prayer more than anything else. Look to Him before you get up in the morning and, when you are up, have a quiet time at once. See, if possible, that it is unhurried. Make it a talk and walk with Him, tell him all, discuss the day with him. Pray for others. Remember: "What things so ever ye desire, when ye pray, believe that ye receive them, and ye shall have them" (Mark 11: 24). Prayer is *most* important.

'*Bible Reading*. It is through His word that God speaks to us. Read carefully and prayerfully (always pray before reading and pray after), and ask Him to open your eyes. Bible Reading is the food for the Christian life (1 Peter 2: 2).

'*Temptation*. "God is faithful, who will not allow you to be tempted above that ye are able; but will with the temptation also make a way to escape" (1 Corinthians 10: 13).

'*The Secret of the Christian Life*. Abiding in Jesus (John 15) and *Faith* (Hebrews 11: 6).

'*Service*. "Let *your light so shine* before men that they may see your good works, and glorify your Father which is in heaven" (Matthew 5: 16). Witness for Jesus by glorifying Him in all you do.

'All the above advice, given humbly and in love, *does not* apply if you have not come to Jesus and surrendered your life to Him.

'Have you done that now? If not, do it, I beseech you, *Now*. It is a matter of life and death. Which will you choose? "I give unto them eternal life, and they shall never perish (John, 10: 28). But "the wages of sin is death" (Romans 6: 23).

'Jesus Christ is longing for you to come to Him but can do nothing until you do. Will you come? Will you *Admit your need, Believe that Christ died for you*, and *Come to him*?

'Remember, it is not a question of feelings. If you say "Come, Lord *Jesus*", He will come, even if you don't at once feel His presence.

'Michael, you don't know what you have missed in not coming to Jesus. My greatest regret is that I didn't come sooner. "Oh taste and see that the Lord is Good: blessed (happy) is the man that trusteth in him" (Psalm 34: 8). The Christian life is one of joy, and can be lived by *anyone* if he fulfils the simple conditions. Will you come and be His witness?'

After mentioning a few people known to Michael personally or by repute, who were believers in this deeper sense, I ended (apart from a string of postscripts repeating some of my points): 'Well, I have been frank. I have told you "the truth, and nothing but the truth". May Jesus come into *your* heart!

'How grand that you should be coming to Tilford. Did you know that "All things work together for good for them that love *him*" (Romans 8: 28)? We shall meet soon, I hope. How I pray that you will be with me, a son of God when we meet.

'Now I must close, for it is getting late. Part of this letter has been written by candlelight, for the lights failed in tonight's raid.

'Much love to you, from *John*.'

7

'A Different Drum'

Michael read the letter again, looking up all the Bible references. And then he 'opened the door'.

In February I had argued, struggled, resisted. Michael in October, like the Apostle John, simply 'saw, and believed'. I had taken days to admit that doing my best could never win the favour of the utterly holy God; Michael recognised the obvious instantly. And Christ's death on the cross, which had mystified him as much as me, suddenly made sense: he felt the force of the familiar words I quoted him from Isaiah: 'All we like sheep have gone astray . . . and the Lord hath laid on him the iniquity of us all.'

When I wrote, 'It is so *simple* that thousands just don't believe it,' Michael did. When I expounded Romans 6: 23: 'The wages of sin is *death*; but the *gift* of God is eternal life through Jesus Christ our Lord,' he wanted that gift, for he saw that the gift was Christ Himself. When I took him to, 'Behold I stand at the door . . .' he became aware without any doubt that Christ stood knocking.

A few days later, during a half-holiday at Charterhouse, another boy called out that my brother was downstairs. I asked, 'Navy or Army?' 'Army.' I rushed down. We walked out together and I wondered what would come. We chatted on this and that, and then Michael said: 'You know that letter of yours? Well, I took the step you wrote about. And I agree: *He* makes all the difference.'

Although unpremeditated, the 'step' was definite. 'There comes a time,' Michael commented to me some months later, 'when a man must take the plunge himself. I could never have come to Jesus *merely* by your and your friends' prayers, although I could never have done without them.'

The implications rather bewildered him at first, and the way he worked them out in wartime has a timeless fascination.

The Regiment's move to Surrey enabled us to see more of each other than at any time since 1939: he could slip over to Charterhouse on my half-holidays and occasionally I lunched at Greengates, the rather ugly house on the edge of Tilford Common which was 'A' Squadron Officers' Mess: my most vivid memory, regrettably, is of the second-in-command's black labrador being sick under the table.

On one field day the Charterhouse Officers' Training Corps did an exercise with the Bays on Frensham Common; we got in Michael's and everyone's way with happy zeal. And on Founder's Day in December 1940, nine days before his twenty-first birthday, Michael was one of several older brothers in uniform who joined us for the house feast. 'After dinner,' recalled Birley, the housemaster, 'we had a kind of sing-song and in no time at all Michael had the baton and was conducting the whole house so that it sang as it had never done before.'

With Michael so near we could explore the Christian way together, and his balanced personality and his better understanding of people were important to my own growth. He met the two friends who had helped me, Derek and Richard. Moreover Richard's brother, tall, thin Tom Butler-Stoney, was a gunner subaltern (11th Royal Horse Artillery) in the same Brigade, 2nd Armoured. At Charterhouse Michael had not appreciated Tom – quiet, rather shy, and known to be a Christian – but now they became fast friends and discussed problems freely.

Tom, Richard and I introduced Michael to a most unusual retired gunner officer who lived nearby at Guildford – Captain Hartley Holmes, a Travelling Secretary of the Officers' Christian Union. Hartley was born in Canada but had served in the British Army until a bad gassing in the First World War. This had turned his thick hair prematurely white, and given him a venerable look though he was only in his fifties with a merry heart. He and his wife and their youngest daughter kept open house at Iron Latch in the Great Quarry at Guildford, where officers cheerfully ate the cupboards bare.

Michael took to the Holmes at once, not least because they liked music and books, and were happy and lively: 'There's an electric atmosphere in that house,' he would say. Under Hartley's inimitable guidance he began to find his way about the Bible and meet other young officers who were active Christians. His faith grew fast.

To cut down travelling time Michael astonished the subalterns at Tilford by buying an old green Humber. Second-hand cars in 1940 were expensive and adventurous. 'We wondered,' recalled Douglas MacCallan, 'if Michael's limited mechanical knowledge and purse could together keep the car on the road.' He would arrive at Charterhouse on half-holidays and drive me over to the Holmes': I blush to think of the home-made cakes I consumed in those days of rationing.

The other officers in the Squadron were beginning to detect a change in Michael. He had always been cheerful and efficient, so they did not at first notice the new happiness and increasing purpose which were obvious to him and to me; but 'he appeared more withdrawn,' recalled Gordon Anthony. 'He seemed to lose his previous young gaiety and to take life very much more seriously. As if he had suddenly realised that what was going on was serious and that it was causing great suffering in the world.' Douglas MacCallan remembered that, 'It all became part of the accepted picture of Michael as standing just a little apart from the robust crudities of his full blooded contemporaries.'

Like most young cavalry officers they could be wild in their gaiety. Every Thursday evening the Squadron Mess at Greengates, Tilford, kept open house. Michael preferred to slip away.

Nearby in Farnham lived a Mrs Deakin, and with her an elderly irrepressible Irishwoman, Helen Peirce, whose girth (she suffered from dropsy) was as memorable as her wit, and her anecdotes as lively as her faith. Helen Peirce was in her early seventies and had retired after a lifetime's devotion to Army Welfare. As a young woman she had opened a Welcome hut at one of the bleakest barracks in dreary country to the west of Dublin: the soldiers' only regret in leaving was that they could no longer go for tea and cakes, and a read or a chat in 'Peircee's' hut. In 1908 she moved to Aldershot, assisting the celebrated Miss Sandes at her Soldiers' Home, and as librarian at Cambridge Hospital. She had worked closely with chaplains and nurses, and was greatly loved by all ranks. She was Irish through and through. Michael, with his love of laughter and good stories, found 'Aunt Peircee' a delight. 'He used suddenly to appear about seven in the evening,' Mrs Deakin wrote, 'and stay to dinner and sit in front of the fire, talking away. I grew very fond of him, he was so young and cheery.'

This 'cheery' spirit helped to prevent any barrier rising between Michael and the men of his Troop, or the Squadron officers. 'Michael's great success,' recalled Peter Willett, the distinguished racing journalist, 'was in adhering rigidly to his own standards without appearing to be prudish or self-righteous, and without condemning those possessing fewer moral scruples. He seemed to be a most serenely happy person, secure in his faith, reliable, giving and inspiring affection.' The change seemed primarily to bring out the qualities which already had made him popular: his charm, his patience, and his kindliness. Michael had never forgotten a face; now he never forgot a birthday. In the dreariness of wartime it is particularly pleasant for an officer or ranker to discover that at least one person wishes 'many happy returns'.

But he seemed to get a little deafer. The slightly deaf can slip into not hearing what they do not want to hear. The Squadron second-in-command, Jimmy Dance, afterwards Conservative MP for Bromsgrove, remembered noticing Michael 'shudder at some of the more ribald remarks made in the Mess'. Unconsciously he began to take the easy way out. His Squadron

Leader, the tall, elegant, imperturbable and popular Alex Barclay, put it nicely: 'I never fathomed in our early days together to what extent his deafness separated him from the gay insouciance of the young cavalry officer, but of one thing I am certain, he was listening to a different drum.'

In late February Winston Churchill brought General de Gaulle and General Sikorski to watch the Bays demonstrate their Cruiser tanks. A week or two later Michael unwittingly acquired some Regimental fame.

The Bays were on a night exercise in the blackout, driving without lights through the darkened country-side and unlit towns from Surrey to the south coast, with Michael's tank leading the column. Since all signposts had been removed during the invasion scare, Military Police had marked the route at each fork or crossroads by placing a blue lamp on the right of the intended route; whenever Michael saw a blue lamp his driver must be sure to keep to its left. In this way the Regiment rumbled successfully into Sussex, negotiating road junctions and fast-asleep country towns.

Suddenly those behind heard a crash, followed by a cascade of broken glass. The column ground to a halt. Headquarters dashed forward and found Michael's tank embedded in a butcher's shop, with the butcher and his wife in night-caps looking out of an upper window to see what had hit them. Michael had duly driven to the left of a blue lamp; only this time the Military Police had placed it on the *left* pavement instead of the right!

In March came Michael's turn for a course at the Tank School at Bovington in Dorset. About a week later Gordon Anthony, one of the other two Old Carthusians in 'A' Squadron, came down unexpectedly from Tilford to join the course.

'I was delighted to see him,' Michael wrote to me. 'We did a bit of swapping of rooms and now we share, which is a great thing. It's going to be very interesting. Today he produced a little pocket Testament. He said he never left it behind, but I've certainly never seen it before. Of course I have not got going with him yet; I shall have to be very careful. I showed him *my* pocket T. – all marked etc., and said I always carried it everywhere. I think he may have been impressed slightly. Anyway, he sees me kneel down at night and in the morning, and I have my Scripture Union calendar on the table.'

Pocket Testaments were easy to obtain, often in waterproof covers, issued by the padres on request; many officers and men carried them. Few probably marked verses, or filled spare pages with notes, as Michael did; his pocket Testament has often come with me on mountain treks and I rejoice in Michael's markings.

'Gordon,' continued Michael in his letter of March 1941, 'is the most charming of people and although he swears as much as anyone, he'll grow out of it, and bit by bit – I believe – he will come to the Lord Jesus. But I must pray, pray, pray – and in the meantime not do too much without Gordon sort-of-asking for it, if you see what I mean.'

After the war Gordon rose to be managing director of Harrods. Some years before his death while still in his fifties, an indirect result of war wounds, he had made an interesting comment, not having seen that letter: 'Michael was not a proselytiser but let everyone know where he stood. His attitude was, "It's all here if you want it." ' Another officer confirmed this: he could not recall Michael bringing up the subject but 'He would state his convictions fearlessly if the conversation turned to religion. It was well known to everyone that he had such feelings.'

He wanted to do more, but recoiled from bulldozing anybody into belief. Moreover, he realised that he might shoot his bolt too soon in a closed community like a Squadron Mess; as he wrote in a military metaphor about somebody else: 'Frontier clashes would damage our whole plan . . . We have given very little time to prayer, without which we can do nothing. We must wait. On the other hand, that's where Hartley's story of the devils comes in. The clever devil said, "Tell them there's plenty of time." ' Michael's desire was constant: 'Pray that I may open his eyes and show him the Way of Life through the Lord Jesus,' he wrote to me about one officer.

If shyness and a sensitive spirit hindered Michael in talking about sacred matters, writing was easier: 'You can say a hundred more important things in a letter than you can in a conversation.' He began writing round, and soon could comment: 'It's a grand life, this. One by one I am telling my friends how I look upon life these days. How I hope I may be of use to Him in telling them something of His Word.'

If a friend was killed before Michael could write, he was disturbed. An Old Carthusian who had been a frequent lunch companion during their year in the City, and had been commissioned in another cavalry regiment, was killed in a London air raid. 'It is so difficult to know about these things,' Michael wrote. 'For the whole of the rest of the day that I saw about Trevor's death, I was troubled and felt rather miserable.

I kept thinking, though, that he'd be going to a better life – but then I don't know anything about Trevor's beliefs. His mother and father had put after his death (in *The Times*) "Thy Will be Done", but you cannot tell what they or he thought. It seems as if he could have done so much in this world, he was so kind and good and helpful. But then – it *was* His will, obviously. I began to feel that I oughtn't to be so dreadfully miserable – and yet, the Lord Jesus wept when he saw Lazarus.'

8

'Such Abounding Joy'

Tom Streatfeild-Moore, who was a descendant of Elizabeth Fry, the prison reformer, might have been a latter-day Siegfried Sassoon had he survived the war, for his twin passions were poetry and horses. He had been Michael's closest friend in Saunderites, and my fagmaster, and was now at Oxford before going into the Grenadier Guards, in which he was badly wounded in action; he recovered, only to be killed in a road accident in Italy after the German surrender, when serving as ADC to General John Harding, the future Field Marshal.

Michael wrote to Tom first of all his friends. After several letters had passed between Bovington and Oxford, Michael told me: 'I had a grand letter from Tom S-M. He's a good way off at present, but certainly nearer to *Him* than ever he was before. This was in answer to my last one which was the strongest I had ever written to him.'

Tom assured Michael: 'Don't distress yourself about me. Leave me to think, and perhaps one day I shall tell you that I am clear about it . . . Quite frankly, it's just God that troubles and upsets me; I can't get Him fixed up at all; He is a nuisance (I didn't mean to be profane! – only He is). I do like your letters. So keep writing.'

Michael wrote freely, and a month later Tom remarked, 'It's most striking how your letters have improved since this "ramp" of yours started. Improved not only in substance but in *style*! I think it's because you've gained confidence in yourself and this confidence has grown (probably quite unconsciously) into your writing.' The style indeed improved, though the earlier letters are still boyish, with overwork of contemporary superlatives like 'frightfully', 'awfully' and 'grand'.

For his birthday, Michael gave Tom George Seaver's biography of Edmund Wilson, the naturalist and doctor who had died with Scott in the Antarctic. Tom enjoyed the book because it made him recall Switzerland where 'one feels oneself more than anywhere else in the hand of God'. After this, Michael was: '. . . full of optimism about Tom. He has knowledge of beauty, a passion for the really lovely things in this world. Edmund Wilson (although he may not have gone the whole way) found his God among the bitterly cold snow and ice of the South Pole. Tom is finding his in the rolling downland of the hills round Compton, and in happy memories of his beloved Switzerland. He will in time, we hope, find something better – his Lord and Saviour.'

When opportunity came to spend a day with Tom, Michael reported: 'I went to see Tom S-M last Sunday; he was on weekend leave from Oxford. Tom's definitely beginning to get hungry, but my greatest difficulty is trying to explain things to him. It's hard. Nor does his present situation exactly help him. But I gave him a New Testament and hope he will have time to read bits.

'He's probably getting some leave in August, during which time I feel there would be a grand opportunity for putting it across. I am starting a big prayer campaign so that he might really accept the Lord. I know he will do eventually, but as you say it comes to different people in different ways.'

Michael had sent him *The Reason Why*, a famous booklet of the day which had wide influence among professional and business people, 'but I do not think it was exactly what he wanted. I feel it might help if I sent him your original letter to me – but I shall wait till his leave in August, when he has more time to concentrate.'

At the large Officers' Mess at Bovington Michael could easily slip away to his room to write, being uninterested in the traditional cavalry amusements of wartime, which a Bay lightly described as 'booze, birds and betting'. In the daytime Michael applied himself to the tank course. The mechanics did not come naturally; the tactics of tank warfare appealed more, especially so that he could pass his knowledge to his Troop when he returned to the Regiment; but he acquired no particular merit. My friend Derek, during his pre-officer training in the ranks ('the toughest course in the country') after a year at university, wrote that a Christian must be the best soldier in his platoon, 'the best athlete, the fittest physically, the one with the most guts and go, the toughest, the one who keeps going all the time, however absolutely beaten he may be. If he is all that, and then knows how to lead others to Christ, he is going to be a great Christian.'

This he-man approach was in character with Derek's powerful physique and personality; it was not Michael's way. He took seriously St Paul's injunction, 'Whatsoever ye do, do it heartily, as to the Lord, and not unto men' (Colossians 3: 23), but he did not strive for primacy, only to do his duty as efficiently as he could.

For weekends he was delighted to find an Old Carthusian friend in civilian war-work near Bovington. Michael felt none of the diffidence which hampered him in the Squadron Mess: 'I got talking with him about what I wanted to when we were walking on top of the golf course. It was the first time I had seen him since October's events, so it meant everything. I went at it, and I know he was impressed. And yet he just hasn't got enough faith to be able to say, "Lord, come into my heart," and believe that He has come. He knows now everything I am getting from this new birth, and I feel he understands fully, but it just ends on the very threshold. It will come in the end, but it may be some time. I know he's worried about himself, but I cannot see how I can do more save pray, pray, pray. There comes a time when a man must take the plunge himself . . .'

Michael's prayers were answered, though not in his lifetime. His friend could write: 'It was Michael's great capacity to pass on his discovery in such a way as to make you want to have a share in what he found. It was Michael's help and encouragement that has given me my faith. Whilst not going the whole way with his views, I am sure I would still be in a complete wilderness if he hadn't started me off.'

And this friend's further remarks accurately sum up Michael's first six months after 'October's events': 'His faith developed very quickly. As it grew, Michael changed and this stood out in his character and all his actions; but it in no way removed from him his sparkle and openness and great friendliness. So often if someone becomes dedicated to a cause, something is lost to those who don't follow exactly parallel lines. It is a sign of greatness not to become isolated from the rest of the world in the interest of your cause.'

When Michael rejoined the Regiment in August 1941 the Bays were sure they would soon be sent somewhere in the Middle East, for many units had been diverted to the abortive Greek campaign and Tobruk was under siege; but the war still seemed far away and Michael could have some halcyon times.

One was a brief visit to the beloved aunts at Park Corner, which was only some twenty miles from Tilford (and, from my point of view two years later, about the same from the Guards' Training Battalion at Pirbright: I recall making them the object of a Brigade Squad motor-cycle run two years later; our corporal-instructor took tea in the kitchen with Mrs Maynard while the delighted aunts entertained a gaggle of guardsman-cadets.) The aunts were too old for war-work and did their best to promote morale by letter writing, good works and hospitality.

Michael set off to Park Corner for Easter 1941. His green Humber was off the road, either from the limitations of his purse or of his mechanical knowledge, and a friend dropped him at Basingstoke, then still a sleepy market town. The mode of progress for soldiers on leave in 1941 was to walk a little way out of a town on the right road and then wait, perhaps ten or fifteen minutes, for the next car or lorry. Michael needed the road for Reading.

'I chanced,' he wrote, 'to approach a little man in the centre of the square to ask him the way. I noticed out of the corner of my eye that he had a small "store" like you see in any market, but this store was full of nothing but booklets, pocket Testaments, quotations and the like. On the side, put up so that everybody could see, were placards in largish letters with such words as "Repent Now", "Come Unto Me", etc. I quickly finished my question about the direction of Reading. Here was something else; here was an instance of a man openly telling people what he thought. The conversation that ensued can be imagined. It was grand . . .'

Michael went on his way, rejoicing: 'How wonderful He is in the amazing ways He gives us such abounding Joy!

'My stay at Park Corner was very short but very enjoyable. I took the opportunity of going out into the woods before breakfast and walking with the Lord. Everything was peaceful save the occasional twitter of the birds in the surrounding trees, or the scamper of a rabbit across my path. How wonderful to be alone with Him, and in such peacefulness.'

Then came an entirely unpremeditated idyll. 'There's a terrific craze for football in the Squadron at present,' Michael wrote home on 18 May, 'and the men get frightfully excited about the matches, which are inter-Troop. Whilst playing football for my Troop, I either tripped up or was thinking of something else while running(!) and went straight over my ankle, spraining it – a thing I've never done before.'

The Medical Officer, Major McGill, drove him over

to Aldershot for an X-ray next day. No bones were broken but he must sit still for a week. As home in Hertfordshire was too far for the petrol allowance and Michael could not manage a train, 'the Doc' asked if he had any friends nearer. Michael telephoned the Hartley Holmes, who responded magnificently. McGill brought him to Iron Latch. 'I'm frightfully lucky to be able to be here,' Michael's letter continues, 'as they are so awfully nice and I'm being fearfully spoilt and having everything done for me. In actual fact, of course, this is necessary because I can't use the right leg but only *hop*! But I use a couple of sticks.

'They've got a very pleasant little garden, so I can make full use of it and sit out all day long. Especially since the weather is simply superb, so it's not being wasted on me. Certainly if one has got to be a sick man this is the way to do it! It's rather annoying being suddenly cooped up like this as there is plenty to do in the Squadron, and I hate being inactive. But since I've got to be inactive I'm going to make the most of it and read a lot, write letters etc. I have plenty of books and the Holmes have plenty more.'

I came over to tea in the garden from Charterhouse on the Saturday. An American, Colonel (later General) Kroner, over on a military mission, though not in uniform since America was still neutral, was staying the weekend with the Holmes. A leading member of the Officers' Christian Union, he was the first American we Pollocks had met. Kroner's friendliness and advice and his exuberant faith greatly impressed Michael, while the Bible studies with the Hartley Holmes, and the books they lent, deepened and strengthened him: it all seemed a providential preparation for the strains and dangers ahead.

9

Last Months in England

Within a few days of Michael's return to duty the Regiment left Surrey and went back to the Wiltshire Downs, this time to the neighbourhood of Marlborough. They moved in convoy on 2 June, Michael 'much enjoying myself on my motor bike, and dashing to the front of the convoy, stopping and then watching it all pass.' An advance party had done wonders, transforming stables, farm cottages and barns in the village of Ogbourne St George so that 'A' Squadron had one of the best billets in the Brigade.

Michael was hoping for a room of his own. 'Needless to say,' he wrote to me on 7 June, 'thanks to your prayers, the Lord had been on before me. I have my little room just like Tilford, except it's bigger. It really is wonderful that I should get a room to myself again, and it does make such a difference, as you can imagine. I've got my books and a table and I can do all the studying I wish.' He was exploring the Bible as never before, and reading *The Pilgrim's Progress*, but the electric light was generated by petrol engine, and weak, 'so I can never do much reading after it gets dark. I try, though, to go upstairs immediately after dinner and so get a good time. But it is certainly good in the morning, although sometimes I don't wake up till 7.30, which is a bad habit – although this is a sleepy place.'

Much of his strength lay in this early discovery of the essential role of a quiet time for Bible reading and prayer, and it would stand him in good stead when placid Ogbourne St George was a distant memory.

Soon the Squadron gave a 'Warming' party, much like any wartime wild fling in the cavalry. 'I couldn't go out,' Michael wrote, 'because I was Orderly Officer. The Padre came in so I talked to him and to one or two very nice neighbours (one of which gives some of us baths as our bathroom hasn't been put in yet!). But I knew that the usual rowdiness would start sooner or later and sure enough it did, but it wasn't long before I was off to inspect the Guard. On the way I met some of our sergeants who were also having a "do", and they said I must come in and see them.

'I think it would have hurt their feelings terribly if I hadn't, but I spent most of my time talking to our Regimental Sergeant-Major, who was at Sandhurst when we were there. Isn't it wonderful how the Lord provides? But it shows how careful one must be. If I had had a really weak mind they would have got me drunk in no time, but by skilful moves I only drank very little beer and at the same time didn't hurt their feelings. Inside (they have a particularly good Sergeants' Mess here) there was much shouting and dancing to the accompaniment of a band.

'Funnily enough, the sergeants' fun and games with all the locals (they soon got on good terms with them!) didn't make me feel half so sick as watching the officers do the same thing. I think it's because one would expect the officers to know better and to be slightly more intelligent. But apparently this is not so, and I can well remember enjoying such rowdy affairs before my "Birthday".' If Michael was inwardly feeling a touch of the intolerance of youth, his brother-officers were unaware of his disapproval at the time; not that they would have loved him the less. Perhaps this was the occasion when some of them dived fully dressed into the local stream!

Major Alex Barclay, the Squadron Leader, liked parties (too much, for some of his superiors) and was very rich as well as popular and brave, and keen on jazz. Having come back from retirement, he had no ambitions for high rank, though later in the war he became a highly regarded commanding officer of the Bays. Barclay had endless care for his men (and in battle would never waste a life) and soon after the Bays had arrived at Marlborough he decided to appoint a Squadron Welfare Officer and asked Michael to take the post in addition to normal Troop duties.

Michael's relations with his Troop had continued good, for the men appreciated his fairness and patience. The shift in his character had set up a slight temporary tension: he had always been a non-smoker and moderate drinker but those who found that smut, sex and profanity were not now encouraged in the slightly limited range of his hearing thought him a trifle dull. This was soon offset. As Jackie Harman, then a senior subaltern in the Squadron, and afterwards General Sir

Jack Harman GCB, OBE, MC, wrote later: 'Michael had a deep sense of compassion and took endless pains on behalf of his men, by whom he was particularly well liked.' A trooper who was for a short time his soldier-servant, E. J. R. Avery, afterwards a transport manager in Plymouth, confirmed this: 'He did a lot for them. For instance he would always write if there was trouble at home – if they were in difficulty, or ill.' And (as a civilian neighbour noticed) 'he was the same to people of all sorts and conditions.'

Welfare was the outlet Michael needed, consuming much time on top of training and exercises. Moreover the Area Welfare Officer was none other than his old headmaster, the founder of St Peter's, Seaford, Rolf Henderson.

'I've started a huge new Social Scheme here,' Michael wrote on 26 June 1941, 'which is a terrific success. A corporal suggested we should have a rambling club and a little later another fellow suggested a debating club. I was so interested with the ideas that I took them up at once and we formed a committee, about seven or eight NCOs or men, with me as chairman and the Squadron Clerk as Hon. Sec. You've no idea how keen these men are and it only wants a small spark to set them really alight with eagerness to get on with the job. We now have dart and table tennis competitions, rambles, cycling games, debates, dances, spelling bees. We are also going to have educational talks and I'm going to get *Major* R. K. Henderson to get some Marlborough masters to come out and give talks.

'The debates are *real* fun – organised in the usual way . . . We debate about once a week in a neighbouring field when it's fine. I had over thirty chaps on Monday debating from 9.15 to 11.20 on: ''That in the opinion of this house the Countryman is a happier and more contented individual than the Townsman." You would be surprised at some of the things said. I'm chairman, which is very interesting. There are some jolly good speakers in the Squadron . . . I also put up newspaper cuttings in the Mess Room – interesting titbits out of *The Times* and *Telegraph* which they probably don't see otherwise . . .

'I do thank the Lord for instilling in me such keenness for something which is often sadly neglected by officers. The great thing is, my Squadron Leader is terribly pleased about it and is backing it all up right and left.'

R. K. Henderson wrote afterwards to my father: 'I know how his men adored Michael. He did so much for them. I remember a walk over the Downs with Michael, planning out a scouting game for the men on the lines we used to play at St Peter's. I remember talking over subjects for Michael's Discussion Group which he ran with great success. He was always thinking out something new to interest them. His standards were of the highest and his men could not help admiring and loving such a character.' In another letter, looking back both to St Peter's and to these months at Marlborough, Henderson added: 'If I may pick out one trait in a most beautiful character, it is the sense of honour which Michael always showed. He had the highest standard of personal integrity of any boy I have known.'

The secretary to the Social Scheme, Lance-Corporal Jack Missen, the Squadron Clerk, was the first Other Rank in the Regiment with whom Michael had a talk about Christ. Michael described Missen as: '. . . intelligent and has always been a churchgoer – chiefly because his mother likes him to. The Lord was wonderful and I had no difficulty in putting it across. I suppose we chatted for half-an-hour. He said he never realised I went as deep as that. He understands now how I am always able to appear smiling and cheerful. He said he'd never heard me swear. It shows how much these things are noticed, doesn't it?'

Michael gave the lance-corporal some small booklets and an underlined edition of St John's Gospel: 'How I jumped for joy when I went to bed that night. It makes me eager to get going on the next. I'm still waiting for an opportunity to speak with the chap Hartley met in the train, but haven't had a chance yet. The Lord will show me when.

'"Oh, worship the Lord in the Beauty of Holiness". Isn't Psalm 46 a grand piece of writing? "God is in the midst of her; she shall not be moved . . . The Lord of hosts is with us; the God of Jacob is our Refuge."'

The Padre enlisted Michael's help in starting a branch of Toc H, the international Christian and social service fellowship founded on the Western Front in the First World War by 'Tubby' Clayton: Michael Halsted in 'C' Squadron had been a keen Toc H member since his Oxford days, but the branch does not seem to have taken off.

The Padre, Basil Morson (later the Reverend Prebendary J. B. Morson OBE, MC, TD, Rector of Wem in Shropshire) was then in his mid-thirties. Tall, a little ungainly, he was not at first easy to know, for Lincoln Theological College and a senior curacy in Shropshire formed a different background from Sandhurst and a commission in the Bays. But Morson was to gain a strong reputation for bravery and devotion to duty. As one officer recalled: 'I first acquired my very real admiration for his qualities when during one battle I assisted him in removing the dead body of a brother officer from a tank; he was clearly of much tougher moral fibre than I.'

Padre Morson was to remain a warm friend to the Regiment. He and Michael were in different traditions of Anglicanism but their friendship and mutual respect deepened steadily, and Michael made a particular point of attending the weekly celebration of Holy Communion.

Yet the daily times by himself meant most: '. . . the early mornings for prayer before many are astir – not that it's ever *very* early. Then I go for a walk on to the surrounding hills before breakfast . . . Much too often am I burdened by the problems of the day and forget Him in the middle of them, but I must try to get to bed early and so have longer Quiet Times . . . Still, the Lord's wonderful even when I have very little time with Him, as during these exercises.'

Michael ended that letter: 'I praise the Lord again for all His goodness. Those Psalms are grand. I love that "Oh that men would 'praise' the Lord . . ."' He underlined the word 'praise' three times: it was his theme for the rest of his life.

And he gave me a new book, the life of Bishop Taylor Smith, who had been Chaplain-General for twenty-three years; on the fly-leaf Michael picked out a quotation from the Bishop: *They that live in Christ Jesus never see each other for the last time.'*

Part Two

NEVER THE LAST TIME

**'They that live in Christ Jesus never
see each other for the last time'**

Bishop J. Taylor Smith, 1860–1938
Chaplain-General, 1901–25

Part

NEARER THE LAST TIME

10

In Convoy

The King and Queen had inspected the 1st Armoured Division in July. In September 1941 Queen Elizabeth came back and inspected the Queen's Bays and took the salute at the farewell march-past on the 1st Eleven cricket ground of Marlborough College. Later Michael and all the other officers were introduced, and they lunched with their Colonel-in-Chief.

Then Michael went in command of a detachment to supervise the loading of the tanks on to freighters at Birkenhead, and returned with fifty-two men in a crowded train to Marlborough. A few nights later the Regiment travelled overnight by train. No junior officer knew where they were bound until they disembarked at Gourock on the shores of the Firth of Clyde, and were taken out to a small but new troopship, ready for her maiden voyage.

Empire Pride, owned by the government and managed by the Bibby Line, was commanded by Captain C. Fountain. It was only 9,247 tons, compared with the 13,000 tons of the Union Castle liners and the 73,000 tons of the *Queen Mary*. *Empire Pride* was supposed to take 1,190 passengers but nearly another thousand were squeezed in: on later voyages she took as many as 3,500, to the considerable discomfort of the troops. Everything was bright and new, with smart Indian stewards. 'From the officers' point of view,' wrote Michael, 'accommodation is very good – with a Dining Saloon and a Smoke Room above, three to a cabin, baths and excellent food. The men's quarters, though, are not so good. That is to say they *would* be good if they were not so crowded. They sleep and eat in exactly the same place and they have to sling their hammocks almost on top of each other. But most of them like the hammocks: in fact Corporal Webb told me he slept all through the night for the first time in the army!' Others disliked them, and the overcrowded quarters; many 'lounge around miserably,' Halsted recorded, 'leaning over the rail, thinking of home and writing letters'.*

The Bays was the only Regiment on *Empire Pride*, which also shipped the divisional signals and medicals, the 2nd Brigade headquarters with Brigadier Raymond Briggs; and Ermyntrude, Alex Barclay's long-haired dachshund – the one female on board. Ermyntrude went all through the North Africa campaign, astonishing General Sir Willoughby Norrie when he met her in the desert: his wife had bred her. Ermyntrude died in Algiers of a stomach complaint.

The Bays now knew that their 1st Armoured Division was to sail round the Cape to North Africa, unlike the previous convoy which had been sent daringly through the Mediterranean. Michael, like any young man before the days of jumbo jets and instant television, looked

---

* *Shots in the Sand*, Michael Halsted, Gooday Publishers, East Wittering, West Sussex, 1990, p. 39.

forward to a great adventure; at twenty-one he would see colourful countries he could not otherwise hope to visit – if their troopship were not torpedoed.

Empire Pride stayed for more than a week in the Firth of Clyde, surrounded by the larger liners of the convoy. Michael and the two other officers who shared a cabin – all three were to be killed in action or die of wounds – enjoyed the wonderful food and their comfortable bunks, and the scenery when the rain stopped and the sun shone. 'Sometimes the tops of the mountains were bathed in mist,' wrote Michael, 'but most of it had cleared away by teatime. A gigantic rainbow arched the sea. After dinner I was on "A" deck to see the moon reflected in the water, with the dark Scottish mountains behind.'

With land so near they expected mail, which did not arrive. Books, things ordered for the voyage, every family's pre-sailing letters, all followed afterwards round the Cape. None of them had a letter for months, hope being deferred at each port of call, and their mail did not reach them until they were in Egypt.

The convoy sailed at last on the night of 30 September – nearly forty ships including four large liners, the aircraft carrier HMS *Argus*, a cruiser and several destroyers. To Michael's excitement, one of these was our brother Martin's ship, HMS *Blankney*; Michael could not send a signal but hoped they would meet at a port of call. Martin, as Michael supposed, 'stayed with us for a week or more and it was a great disappointment when he turned back. Still, during that time it was grand to think of him there, and each night my prayers for him seemed more real than ever.'

HMS *Blankney*, being primarily on anti-aircraft duty,

always turned back at the range limit of German shore-based bombers; but Martin had in fact left the ship for another posting, though Michael did not learn this until after arrival in Egypt. The convoy was only threatened once, by a Fokke-Wulf Condor; the gun teams rushed to their guns, the cruiser fired, the aircraft carrier launched a plane and the German hastily flew away.

The Bay of Biscay reduced the Mess decks to a chaos of smell and sprawling troops; many officers retreated to their bunks but Michael was only slightly sick once and never missed a meal. By Sunday 5 October they had turned south into smoother, warmer waters. Michael found more men at Holy Communion than on the previous Sunday. 'The Padre is very pleased and told me that all sorts of people who never used to turn up in England came along today.' The main Sunday service took place later on deck. Michael had been shocked to find 'no place at all on board this ship set aside for worship. I think it is deplorable. They might at least have supplied a small cabin for the purpose. Of course it's all right for me – I've got a cabin with a good deal of privacy and I can have my Quiet Times. But for those of the men who are Christians, it can't be too easy.' Space was at a premium, no cabin could be found for a makeshift chapel, but when the sergeants' saloon proved too small, Holy Communion was transferred to the much larger saloon for officers; 'people of every rank crowded in,' recalled Padre Morson.

One Sunday the record number of fifty communicants attended at 8 a.m.; the main service, entirely voluntary, had been moved to a roomier part of the main deck, with band and choir in the middle. 'The men flock along to the service,' noted Michael. 'For most, I suppose, it breaks the monotony although I hope some really get something from it.' On one occasion in the tropics, when many officers and men had taken to sleeping on deck, the Padre, preaching on prayer, suggested, 'What better time could you have for saying your prayers than when sleeping on deck at night with only the sky above you?'

The voyage had slipped into a routine 'with plenty to laugh at . . . We are a very happy party,' Michael wrote, 'and it is nice to have a good lot of officers, and no one could have a better Colonel.'

Michael's two cabin mates were a good lot, too. Joe Radice, an Oxford man who had been brought up in Switzerland and was fluent in French and Russian, had a rather nervous manner and a tendency to muddle, which made him the butt of some of the others. However, any appearance of being a fool was deceptive; he was quick witted and brave, and when wounded in battle Joe would save the lives of Michael Halsted and others by guiding a lost ambulance to safety despite being in great pain. He was to be killed in 1945 fighting with the French resistance. Chris Parker, the other in Michael's cabin, was son of the editor of *The Field* and lived near Charterhouse. Gordon Anthony recalled him as 'one of the most charming men I have ever met'. It was to Chris that Gordon owed his life when he was wounded. Chris Parker was to be killed in Italy in 1944.

Once the weather became warmer Michael preferred to sleep on deck. His soldier-servant Selby, a Wiltshire man, who found him 'a real gentleman in every way who was very good to me,' put up Michael's camp bed, and 'I usually awake soon after six when the natives come on deck and if you are still asleep tell you politely they wish to wash it. Whereupon if you're sensible you get up, shake yourself, stretch yourself, yawn and gather up your bed and bedding and proceed to your cabin, which is always particularly warm. If you're not sensible – well, the hose is brought into play *whoever* may still choose to sleep on . . .'

Michael would wash and dress, stroll on deck, watching the other ships, then 'lie down on my bed and have a read and a nice quiet time for my prayers. At 7.30 we have Officers P.T. which is rather fun, and we do physical jerks and relay races and what not. When the ship is rolling of course it's not so easy, although more amusing.' After a mouth-watering breakfast 'most mornings are taken up by our Troop Training of which we have done a good deal since the voyage started, and during which we can teach and discuss hundreds of useful things with the men, although of course the most important job of the lot (riding in our vehicles) is hardly possible!'

Every morning they also had a Boat Stations parade, '. . . during which the Captain comes waddling round to see everyone is wearing his life jacket correctly. Then at 1 p.m. lunch, also very good, and afterwards usually more training. Some people like to fall asleep in the afternoon but I never really want to and always find plenty to do. After tea I often read or write letters and the next item is the sunset which is something to look forward to every day. The sunsets are quite remarkable for their beauty, colouring and (as you might as well say) their artistic design. The clouds seem to weave themselves into the most peculiar patterns and for at least an hour after the red ball has actually disappeared, the colours change frequently.' Michael loved sunsets: 'A grand sunset tonight – layer upon layer of thin grey coloured clouds, just lightly bathed in the red glow of the sun as it disappeared over the horizon.'

During dinner, when music was often provided by 'A' Squadron's band, an informal group of seven players organised by Alex Barclay, Michael would thoroughly enjoy the conversation which ranged over all sorts of subjects. Then he would go on deck to look at the stars, and write or read, '. . . but never go to bed very late. Some people like retiring early in the morning, having played cards all night, but I always feel one can occupy oneself in a better way than that! Of course there's no doubt one can get very bored on a boat like this on a long voyage and card games certainly pass away the time. But I've never felt the urge to take part and anyway I want to use the time, not pass it!'

Many were indeed bored, and looked back on the voyage as everlasting: 'You must imagine,' recalled one officer, 'a lot of young, healthy, vigorous men cooped up for some six weeks or so. From 6 p.m. onwards certainly nothing to do except talk, read, play bridge or chess.' There was occasional rowdiness and a good deal of mild gambling, with steady drinking but not much drunkenness, although one poker-playing officer is remembered casually ordering, just before the bar closed, thirty-six whisky-and-sodas to see his table through to the end of the session!

'You know, John,' Michael wrote to me, 'I don't know what it would have been like to come on this trip without my Saviour and Friend. I should probably have ended up gambling and getting drunk and generally wasting my time. As it is I can have constant times of intercession, I can put every problem into His hands, and I can safely know that wherever I go He will be there also. Moreover I am eager to read

books and learn about all the places I may visit, eager
to reap the benefits of this magnificent expedition, not
forgetting to give Him the thanks, the praise and the
glory for it all. I ask His guidance continually for my
work and several prayers for better relations with some
of the NCOs have been well and truly answered. In fact
my Troop couldn't be working better. The prospect of
visiting these far off countries thrills me exceedingly
and I shall never cease to think how much I have to
thank and praise Him for.'

At the end of the last page he added in capitals the
words of the Risen Jesus to His disciples, from the last
verse of St Matthew: 'I am with you always.' Michael
did not mouth texts or lard his speech with pieties:
only in the privacy of his letters did he speak freely
of 'the Lord', and of 'my Saviour and Guide and His
everlasting presence'. Christ's promise, 'I am with you
always,' was focal to his faith, which beyond all else
was a Friendship.

Among the passengers in *Empire Pride* were four colonels of the Royal Engineers going out to Persia, which
had been occupied by Britain and the Soviet Union to
forestall a German invasion through the Caucasus. The
colonels were to change ships at Freetown in Sierra
Leone for Lagos, then fly across Africa and on to
India. One of them was a Colonel Clutterbuck, a
railway expert in his mid-forties, wearing the Third
Afghan War (1919) medal.

Michael and Clutterbuck '. . . got talking after a week
or two, and we used to stand by the rails on deck and
watch the other ships in the convoy and he used to tell
me of his experiences in the Army and elsewhere. He
seemed so ready to talk and such a really interesting

and delightful person, with a broad-minded opinion about everything.

'I prayed at the beginning of the voyage that I might get to know well someone on the ship, but it never really occurred to me that Col. C. would be the person. Often, however, I mentioned religion but only in a very broad sense – once when we were talking about the state of the world and I told him I thought that if every nation based its ideas on Christianity we should never get wars. Each time I did get in any way towards that subject, the conversation would turn away to something else.

'But one memorable time he and I had come up on to deck after dinner and were standing by the rails watching the little waves get swept aside as our ship cut its way through them. It was very warm and the stars amazingly bright, whilst in the dim distance we watched the other liners move forward too. As usual we got talking on every conceivable subject and he asked me whether I had begun to look ahead and plan my life rather than "just skim along the surface", as he put it.

'From there I turned the conversation to the things "that really matter" even though he told me afterwards in his own mind he hadn't meant it that way at all. But I just got going with my story, and in my own rustic, blunt way, I told him what I lived for these days. He seemed immediately interested although at first incredibly puzzled. I told him about your letter, and finally I gave him two booklets. It seemed incredible the way he accepted what I said and wanted more. You can imagine the Joy in my heart when I realised he was hungry and really believed me.

'He read the things I had given him and the next

morning came and sat down at my table at breakfast.
He wanted to see your letter badly, so I gave it to
him. When he returned it at lunchtime he told me
it was the most amazing thing he had ever read and
hoped I didn't mind as he copied out most of it!! The
second person to do so!' [Tom Streatfeild-Moore was
the other: Michael kept the original 'conversion' letter
of October 1940 in his Bible until the end of his life,
when it returned to me.]

The convoy had turned towards West Africa. About
noon on 14 October they saw on the horizon the hills
of Sierra Leone, the colony founded by Wilberforce and
the Slave Trade Abolitionists as a refuge for released
African slaves. Everyone crowded the decks to watch
the escort and troopships manoeuvre into single file as
the convoy entered the estuary which leads to Freetown.
'The water was beautifully calm and shoals of minute
flying fish scurried across the top of the water to get
out of the way of the ship.' Steep hills, with red soil
and thick dark green vegetation, rose abruptly from the
shore. They anchored near Freetown on the southern
shore. A tanker came up, then dozens of small craft,
with natives who amused the troops by diving for
pennies.

Michael stood with Colonel Clutterbuck to watch
the sun 'going down behind a low range of hills,
reflecting on the sky the most wonderful blend of
colouring I've ever seen.' Michael burst into song,
knowing that the Colonel also was musical: 'Then the
conversation turned again to "the things that matter".
It was interesting to hear all he had to say. He had
always told a friend of his in England that she ought
to come to church, but he told me he often felt a beast
as he knew he was a bit of a hypocrite.

'He told me he didn't know how he was going to stick the parting from England and his friends, but "Now," he said, "I have other ideas. I'm not worried now. What have you got for me to read tonight?"' Michael gave him a little New Testament and some further booklets. 'He accepted them with much gratefulness and it seemed wonderful to see the change.'

Two days later 'my dear friend Col. Clutterbuck' had to land with the other Sappers: 'It really has been enjoyable knowing him. Every conversation we had, and we had a fair number, was of the most interesting possible and I certainly learnt a great deal. There never seemed any limit to the variety of subjects he was willing to discuss, and the fact that the difference of age between us was extremely large never seemed to have the slightest effect on the situation. I shall certainly miss him during the remaining weeks of this voyage.

'His handshake at the end was wonderfully firm and he waved to me from his launch as he moved away. I *was* sorry to see him go, but how overjoyed I was to think that the Lord had used me to bring the truth before Col. C's eyes. How I thanked Him that night.'

Months later, in the Western Desert, Michael received 'a charming letter from my Colonel friend. He's in India now, and says he is persevering. I realise how difficult things must be for a man who is getting on in years; it can't be easy to overturn all one's old habits and ideas and begin a new life. He says he is reading a lot of the Word, and I feel sure the Lord is working within him.'

After Michael's death the Colonel wrote me a letter of far more than formal condolence: 'It is very sad that such a fine and outstanding young fellow should be cut down so soon after reaching manhood. I am quite sure though that by his fine example and intense faith he was an inspiration and source of strength to many just as he was to me, and the good that he did in his short life was remarkable . . . The standard he set was so high.' The Colonel told me that he still had his copy of my letter of 1940 to Michael; perhaps that letter began, in a sense, my literary career, although I had no plan to be a writer and my first book would not be written and published until ten years later, shortly before I was ordained.

11

'A New Impetus'

Convoy troops were not allowed ashore as their numbers would have swamped Freetown. Officers and men had little to do except, as Halsted recorded, 'loll about feeling limp and sweaty,' and watch the Sunderland flying boats skimming the water as they took off or touched down, or use binoculars to study the Colonial Empire at work and play.

The men's Mess decks below became almost unbearable for heat and smell, despite wind chutes, while the officers' cabins and saloon had an efficient blower. Michael always regretted the contrast between the comparative luxury of the officers and the discomforts of the men, a hang-over from the nineteenth century when officers came from high social class and most of the men from the poor. However, a few months after the voyage of the *Empire Pride* the Prime Minister's young private secretary, Jock Colville, having at last secured release for active service, went out as an aircraftsman in a troopship to South Africa, and knew at first hand his companions' resentment at the contrast between conditions above and below. He wrote to Churchill, pointing out the political dangers, and in later years of the war the troops were given more space and the officers less.

On the *Empire Pride* Bays officers worked hard to keep their men amused out of the hours of training and fatigue duties by organising entertainments, games and competitions. Michael's first essay competition rather back-fired. He offered two subjects. Most of the Troop chose 'Life at Sea' and used their essay to list 'all the things they don't like about this trip. Still we live and learn, and I shall set a better variety of subjects next time.'

After five days the convoy sailed from Freetown. When they crossed the Equator 'it was hard to believe it as it was quite cool and no sun or heat. The sea was moderate. At tea time we had an amusing ceremony with Father Neptune, his daughter (the ship's adjutant), barbers, constables and Joe Baker* as master of ceremonies.'

By ancient tradition of the sea, anyone on board who had never crossed the Line must undergo (by proxy when there were too many) a boisterous initiation into Neptune's domain as the 'barbers' would splash on thick white 'soap', then shave it off by using wooden scrapers: 'There were about fifteen to twenty victims representing the different units. The Brigadier was the first to be "shaved" and soundly ducked, much to the amusement of the troops who were perched on every conceivable vantage point you could think of. Some tried standing on the rails until they were rightly warned off for "ships don't stop for a man overboard". The Colonel was also a victim. It must have been extremely cold on a day like this.'

---

* Captain G. H. M. Baker, Queen's Bays, killed in the Battle of Gazala, 29 May 1942.

On 30 October, a fortnight after leaving Freetown, Michael's half of the convoy approached Table Bay; the other half went on to Durban: 'I had a quick meal and rushed up on to deck again, just as the sun was beginning to set and the land in front becoming plainer. Soon we could see the white of the houses and buildings of the town and as dusk came down, the whole scene turned into a blaze of lights the likes of which we hadn't seen since before the war. A message was flashed to us from a hill close by, and we could read it to mean that we weren't to enter the harbour till the morning. A pilot's boat came alongside and its skipper bellowed some information through a megaphone. At the end of it he shouted "Carry on, please", at which the troops, now eagerly lining the rails, broke into a roar of delight.

'We anchored that night and the next morning I came up on to deck at 6.30 a.m. to behold the most beautiful sight I had ever seen. There was the town across the water, a mass of modern white buildings, whilst behind rose the hills, their peaks bathed in the morning sunshine. The whole scene seemed so fresh and delightful at this hour of the morning.'

By mid-morning, leave passes were issued to officers and men. Halsted recorded in his diary: 'The Padre, the Doc, Michael Pollock and I step off together. I do not notice my first step on shore, the thought comes to me later, down the dock. The old *Empire Pride* looks quite impressive from the shore, but nothing compared to the *Dominion Monarch* or *Strathaird*. We walk the whole way out of the docks wondering what is in store for us.'* They soon discovered: 'Four consecutive days of

---

* *Shots in the Sand*, p. 49.

inconceivable kindness,' as Michael put it, to everyone
of the convoy: the magnificent welcome and hospitality
which Cape Town extended to British troops throughout
the war. Inhabitants flocked to the docks to make sure
that everyone enjoyed himself.

The Padre telephoned to make contact with the Archbishop of Cape Town, who fortunately was not away
on tour and later confirmed several men of the Bays
whom Padre Morson had been preparing; Archbishop
Derbyshire was 'most friendly and hospitable'. (The
Padre prepared more Confirmation candidates when
the voyage resumed; they had no opportunity of being
confirmed before the campaign but he admitted them
to Communion as 'ready and desirous'.)

After the Padre's telephone call they 'waded into the
shops and amused ourselves picking out presents to
send home,' Michael recorded. After the austerity of
besieged England it 'seemed amazing to us, used to
barely stocked shops with mostly only advertisements
in the windows, to see counters overflowing from top
to bottom with every conceivable commodity. In every
other shop chocolate was in abundance and fruit in
numbers not seen by us for years.'

A stranger suggested Markham's for lunch. They
revelled in the brown bread and butter which came
with the soup, and finished with raspberries and cream.
The manageress came up and said: 'You gentlemen have
been the guests of the gentleman who was sitting at
the next table and has just left. He is a well-known
business man – and has just lost his son.' (Michael did
not record this last remark: the manageress may have
dropped her voice and he missed it.) They were touched
and embarrassed and all signed a note of thanks to be
handed to him when he came next day.

Back in Adderley Street they were approached by a woman who offered them a drive. She was a Mrs Jean Lees, wife of a Scottish doctor at the North African front. She drove them in a little four-seater at such a furious pace that they were relieved when she let Halsted take the wheel once they reached the national road on the outskirts. Mrs Lees, talking all the time about the land and the people, took them to her home at Stellenbosch, through scenery in all its spring freshness, and ended the day by giving them supper in a cinema restaurant, including fresh strawberries and cream.

Next day, with the 9th Lancers and the Rifle Brigade, the Bays marched through the city. The band played too slowly and caused many changes of step, 'but considering we had been on board ship for so long, it wasn't a bad show.' The streets were crowded with spectators. Those of British stock clapped loudly, while Afrikaners gazed silent and unmoved, except for some who smiled: tensions in the South Africa of Smuts did not arise from apartheid (not yet defined as a policy or a philosophy) but from differing attitudes to the British Empire. Yet many of the Afrikaners were actively loyal, and wherever Michael or the others went they would be greeted by strangers of both races who wanted to hear about England and to thank them for their part in defending the Empire.

After the parade Michael lunched with the same three friends, then left them and took a fast local train southwards, with Table Mountain on his right, to the suburb of Kenilworth. He went to look for Captain G. S. Dobbie, listed by the Officers' Christian Union as willing to offer hospitality to passing officers. He was a cousin of the General Dobbie who was winning imperishable fame in the defence of Malta.

Michael found the house, Glenvar, in spacious grounds with several beautiful trees, and a palm tree on the lawn, only to learn that Dobbie was back in the army, stationed up north in the Transvaal. 'But a little housekeeper invited me in to a cup of tea, and said she would ask one of the students in.' The place turned out to be the training home of a small but far flung pioneer mission, the African Evangelistic Band – an offshoot of the Faith Mission based in Scotland and Ireland. The compound included the Garatt Memorial Hall, which later became St James's Church, of the Church of England in South Africa.

Michael stayed on to early supper. 'It was grand to see some Christians again, and they were all so kind and helpful. We all had supper round a large table and there were about ten to twelve of us. It must be a happy place in which to live. We said a short grace before the meal and then sang a very beautiful one at the end. The native servant must have been waiting for this as he entered immediately afterwards to clear away!' There was much laughter at the meal, and since some of the married students had small children, everyone next played progressive ping-pong and other games. Then followed the singing of hymns, 'most of which I didn't know,' and family prayers at which an old lady commented line by line on the twenty-third Psalm. Before Michael left, they had fixed up a sight-seeing tour for next day.

'As I sat in the train on my way back to the ship, I thought of what a wonderful world it might have been and still can be, if everyone had the simply lovable ideas of these kind people.'

Back in the city, as brilliantly lit as London before the war, with the parliament buildings and the cathedral partially flood-lit, he was able to listen to a symphony orchestra in the old City Hall before returning to the docks.

Next day was Sunday. They had early Communion in the ship, then a short morning service on the quayside. 'The band played and we sang hymns as the little tugs kept dashing backwards and forward in the harbour. Numbers of strange birds which we hadn't seen before settled on the rocks nearby and seemed to listen in to our service.'

Then, like everyone else, he enjoyed a long day's hospitality and drive, interspersed with the frequent drinking of tea, a South African habit which amused Michael. The views were magnificent: 'out along the sea coast, with mountains rising steeply on our left and the waves smashing themselves against the rocks on our right. We saw a little sandy bay, used as a fishing harbour, and then we went through vineyards, the road twisting and turning as we sped along . . .'

In the evening he was back at Kenilworth. After supper they took him to the Baptist church at Claremont, a nearby suburb. Michael had never been to a non-Anglican church, and although he loved the Anglican liturgy he enjoyed the Baptist simplicity, 'and it was grand to hear the singing of people who really understood the words. The Pastor was a nice old fellow with a white pointed beard and silvery hair,' but Michael was sitting too far back to hear all the sermon. Pastor Watson and his wife invited him home for yet more cups of tea.

Another guest, also from the convoy, was an officer of the Merchant Navy who was assistant purser of the *Strathaird*: Wilbert Guthrie Watson, from Edinburgh, aged twenty-six. When the time came to leave, the

Pastor said: 'It is good for you two young Christians to go home together.' They got out of the bus at the dock gates and walked 'very slowly along the quayside at about one in the morning, talking hard about our various experiences and exchanging opinions on most Christian subjects. After all, what did *sleep* matter!' The next evening also ended with Wilbert Watson and Michael 'talking hard' as they walked towards the great P & O liner *Strathaird* and the little *Empire Pride*. 'I don't know when I shall see him again,' Michael wrote when at sea again, 'but I can look across to his ship in the daytime and think of him, and pray for him at night.'

On the fourth and last day, Michael went up Table Mountain in the cable car with the Padre, the Doctor and Michael Halsted, to enjoy the famous view. As Halsted noted: 'We could see our "hell ship" in the dock, and rejoiced to be free of it for a time. The Bay looked wonderful and the still blue sea, so very unlike England.'*

That evening Michael slipped back to Kenilworth, a home from home. The appreciation was mutual. One of the hospitable friends he met there was the accountant of the *Cape Argus*, Cecyl Till, a man in his early thirties. He wrote to tell me how 'we very much enjoyed fellowship in Christ with your brother. He was looking very fit and rejoicing in his Lord and Saviour . . . How it must rejoice your heart to hear of your brother's steadfast faith and how faithfully he is testifying of his Saviour in his everyday life.'

The convoy sailed onward to the war during the

---

* *Shots in the Sand*, p. 57.

morning of 4 November, and by the end of the day the land had fallen below the horizon and South Africa had become a memory. 'But what a memory it was. I haven't yet met one officer or man who didn't enjoy every minute of his shore leave, and everyone says they look forward to the time when they can revisit that grand city.' As the Regimental History says, 'No member of the Regiment who was there will ever forget the kindness and hospitality that they received.'

Michael's dominant memory was of 'my *spiritual* experiences. It was a pleasant short spell in dry dock, refitting. The people I met, the conversations we had, the things I saw, have one and all given me a new impetus in my work, a new and even more living encouragement to "put on the whole Armour of God".'

Michael had been a little lonely spiritually. Many officers on board were churchgoers, whether their beliefs were defined or vague; and in 1941 few officers in a regiment such as the Bays would be open unbelievers. But Michael longed that all of them should experience the power of Christ and rejoice in Christ's companionship; to Michael, a Christian was pre-eminently one whose life was delightfully dominated by Christ, who loved Christ and was guided by the Bible, like the simple Christians of Kenilworth.

'I feel it is how He wants it, this great joy and subsequent urging which I find in me when I have met Christians,' he wrote to me. 'We should be able to keep ever faithful even if we do not see Christians for a long time, but when we *do* see them after what seems like a long time, I feel He wants us to get that fresh impetus which I have experienced so often . . .

'I was looking at Galatians 6 the other night and I do think it is such excellent teaching especially for me at the moment whilst I am praying for various officers on board. There is a nice promise too in verse 7 – "Be not deceived; God is not mocked: for whatsoever a man soweth, that shall he also reap." We may say something or do something and perhaps attempt to tell a person about the Lord. We may then go away thinking that we have not succeeded in our object. But we can be sure every little bit does good, and we shall know in the end the result of our sowing.

'And then we have the urging to carry on with our work and (verse 9), "Let us not be weary in well doing; for in due season we shall reap, if we faint not."'

Michael particularly treasured an anonymous meditation on the unsearchable riches of Christ which the Baptist pastor had given him from the weekly printed letter of a Presbyterian minister:

'To the artist, He is the Altogether Lovely; to the architect, He is the Chief Corner Stone; to the astronomer, He is the Sun of Righteousness; to the baker, He is the Living Bread; to the banker, He is the Hidden Treasure; to the biologist, He is Life; to the builder, He is the Sure Foundation.

'To the carpenter, He is the Door; to the doctor, He is the Great Physician; to the farmer, He is the Sower; to the Educationalist, He is the Great Teacher; to the florist, He is the Rose of Sharon; to the geologist, He is the Rock of Ages; to the horticulturist, He is the True Vine; to the judge, He is the Righteous Judge; to the juror, He is the Faithful and True Witness.

'To the jeweller, He is the Pearl of Great Price; to the Lawyer, He is the Counsellor; to the oculist, He is the Light of the Eyes; to the philanthropist, He is the Unspeakable Gift; to the philosopher, He is the Wisdom of God; to the preacher, He is the Word of God; to the railwayman, He is the New and Living Way; to the Sculptor, He is the Living Stone; to the servant, He is the Good Master; to the toiler, he is the Giver of Rest; to the sinner, He is the Lamb of God who taketh away the sins of the world; to the believer, He is the Saviour, Redeemer, and Lord.'

12

Eager for Battle

Nine days after the convoy sailed from Cape Town came an incident which symbolises the irony of war.

The old, historic battle-cruiser HMS *Repulse*, which had been their ocean escort since Table Bay, sailed slowly down the line of ships 'so that everybody could see what she looked like'. Cunningly camouflaged to appear as two ships from a distance, she was a fine sight at one hundred yards. Her crew manned the decks, the Captain in his white uniform stood high above the bridge, field-glasses in hand, strong and silent. The Marine band played, each ship in the convoy dipped in salute as *Repulse* passed, and the cheers of the troops were answered by the cheers of the sailors.

HMS *Repulse* handed over her duties to HMS *Revenge* and sailed across the Indian Ocean to Singapore. Less than one month after the *Empire Pride* had saluted her she and the *Prince of Wales* were sunk by Japanese aircraft off the coast of Malaya, three days after Pearl Harbor.

The *Empire Pride*'s long, slow voyage continued, everyone sad to have left Cape Town 'but glad that we are getting on with the job, so that we can finish it, and get home to our families again'. Michael knew

how much his men missed their families. One evening
with 'a lovely sky, I stood talking to Sgt. Clare on deck
until the moon (almost full) rose above the clouds in front
of us. He's an interesting person, Sgt. Clare. He feels
the parting from home a great deal, I think, as before
he had always been with his wife or not far distant
from her. It's good to have a Troop Sergeant such as
him, and even better to have *two* good ones.' Michael
was delighted when his Squadron Leader, Alex Barclay,
with Ermyntrude at his heels, 'told me he thought we
had trained up my Troop ("a young troop," he put
it) very well – a good compliment to Sgts. Clare and
Brookfield who have worked like niggers. An ideal
example of co-operation.' ('Niggers' in that context had
no derogatory racial overtone in 1941.)

Both sergeants were killed: Clare during the action in
which Michael was wounded, and Brookfield in Italy in
the final battle. Both were tough, but Michael knew that
Clare ended every letter to his wife, 'And don't forget
your prayers.' The embarrassing task of censoring his
men's letters gave him a realisation that under apparent
indifference lay deeper feelings: 'Quite a number of them
say something like "I am sure we can put our trust in
God."'

In the overlong shipboard hours off duty Michael still
found plenty to do, and began to learn Arabic with a
small party of enthusiasts. Every fine evening he found
unfailing pleasure in the sunset. 'We had the best sunset
ever this evening,' he noted as they neared the Horn
of Africa. 'Instead of just a portion of the sky being lit
up, almost the entire scene was a blaze of crimsons and
light blues and dark blues and white and orange. And
all this was reflected in one large pink cloud above us.'
It reminded him of a verse from Ecclesiastes: 'Truly the

light is sweet, and a pleasant thing it is for the eyes to behold the sun' (Ecclesiastes 11: 7).

Another evening he was up on deck, writing a letter: '. . . but stopped to talk to the Padre who came to sit and watch the sunset with me. He asked me whether I'd ever thought of being ordained. I don't know what prompted him to say that. Actually I never try making up my mind on anything I may do after the war, but rather remember a good comment in Psalm 119, verse 105: "Thy word is a lamp unto my feet, and a light unto my path" – a *lamp*, not a searchlight.' If Michael ever seriously considered ordination, or the mission field, or remaining in the army – and Colonel Draffen believed he would have done well in the profession if the deafness had allowed – he never referred to the future in his letters. In 1941 'after the war' seemed a state impossible for a young man to imagine.

The next evening he continued his letter, 'but found myself again carried away with the glory of the setting sun. A little red ball slipping down behind the sea and then the whole sky around and above it lit up with a golden tint. How much have we to thank God for! There are a multitude of things we never remember. "Forget not all His benefits" is certainly good advice.'

They anchored off Aden without shore leave and passed slowly up the Red Sea, hearing the news that General Auchinleck had launched Operation Crusader without waiting for the Bays and the rest of the 1st Armoured Division. Despite heavy British losses, some local defeats and an initial failure to relieve Tobruk, the Eighth Army was pressing Rommel back and regaining lost ground. 'The news of this offensive has had a great effect on everybody, especially the men, who are always asking whether we've heard any more, and of course the result of this attack will have a big effect on what we ourselves do.'

November 23 would be the Bays' last Sunday on *Empire Pride* – a ship which would survive the war, to be renamed *Charlton Pride* in 1954, then *Calgaria* and finally *Embassy* before being broken up in 1964.

They had hymns at Holy Communion, and at the main service on deck. Padre Morson preached on The Good Shepherd and 'made the excellent suggestion that we should all learn the 23rd Psalm and use it as a Prayer.' Then they sang, 'Now thank we all our God', a hymn which officers and men agreed was appropriate at the end of a voyage across dangerous seas with never a U-boat sighted.

They were longing to reach the battle and help throw Rommel out of Africa. Michael wrote to our parents: 'I don't mind telling you I'm extremely happy and contented and looking forward to the future with eagerness. There's no knowing what interesting places we may see and the things we may do, and the more the better as I shall have plenty to tell you when I get back.'

The past gave him confidence in the future, whatever lay ahead in the battle they were soon to join. His mind ran again to that refrain of Psalm 107, one of his favourites; he had underlined verse 8 in red pencil in his pocket New Testament with Psalms: 'Oh that men would praise the Lord for his goodness, and for his wonderful works to the children of men!'

He wrote to Hartley Holmes, whose wisdom, faith and humour had helped so much: 'Often when I'm lying in bed, I think and try to count up all the amazing things the Lord has done for me, and each time I realise how frequently I am inclined to forget to thank Him. Truly since my conversion just over a year ago the multitude of good things that He has done is "past finding out" and I can hardly conceive what I should have done without Him on this ship. "Forget not all His benefits" is indeed necessary advice.

'And the whole of one's life, one's everyday life, seems to fit together like a jigsaw puzzle, each little event coinciding with the next, all part of His wonderful plan.'

The Bays landed at Suez on the afternoon of 25 November 1941 and marched, as dusk fell, to the transit camp. Egyptians left their bazaars and cafés 'to watch us go by as the troops sang their songs and whistled to keep step.'

That night, as Michael curled up in his bed to keep warm, in the tent where all 'A' Squadron officers were together, 'leaving a starlit icy night outside,' the unaccustomed silence, 'no noise of ship's engines or dynamos; just silence,' made it 'easier to thank God for our safe arrival after a long voyage.'

Next morning the Regiment went by train beside the Canal, then across the desert and into the Nile Delta and out into the desert again, to camp near Amriya, ten miles west of Alexandria. Scenes familiar to the thousands who fought and served in Egypt were recorded in detail in Michael's diary: 'the patient oxen pulling the shaft of the well round and round, or hauling the wooden ploughs; the camels everywhere, often trotting along with its rider perched on top rocking from side to side; the donkeys with their load, mostly overloaded. And all the way along, the men and women and children stopped their work, put down their tools and waved to us, often giving the thumbs up sign.'

The sand of the whole camp area had been churned up by troop movements until it blew into clothes and food and bedding, and made Ermyntrude sneeze. The weather was capricious: 'sometimes warm sun burning your neck and making the glare immense; other times cold northeast winds blowing across the camp and making one's lips all rough.' The men were surprised how cold a desert could be, especially at night, and officers went around in a variety of golf-jackets, corduroy trousers and other unmilitary but weatherproof clothes.

Michael shared quarters with four others – and two to come – and wrote up his diary by candlelight at the table in their tent: 'Peter reads a book by Gilbert Murray on Religion, but I wish he would read the Bible instead! Chris is reading *The Leisure of an Egyptian Official* by Lord Edward Cecil' – which, like other books, had passed from hand to hand; Michael had enjoyed it on the ship. Another was writing home and the fourth was washing up his mug and food utensils. 'It is really rather fun here,' Michael wrote home, 'and just the sort of simple life I love. Was it outside a church in Marlborough that I saw this bit of wise advice: "Learn to enjoy the simple things in Life; they cost the least and last the longest."' He ended: 'I want to tell you that I'm really very happy out here and you couldn't have a better set of officers; we are a very happy family. The men too are a grand lot and this makes a huge difference.'

Michael's unfailing cheerfulness, including his amusement – not cynical, perhaps even a little naive – at any difficulty or petty disaster, was one reason for his popularity. Yet this making the best of everything was a characteristic of the Cavalry. Michael Halsted put it well in his diary entry for 26 November: 'The way we eat now is very different from our ship style, but even the most superior officers are as adaptable as any and no one complains at all . . . When it comes to hard living it is not so hard to get down to it.'*

The tanks arrived by rail under command of Gordon Anthony, who was covered with soot from the engine after sleeping in the guard's van. Officers and men were busy from dawn to dusk as they checked and tested guns and started desert training. The ranges were 'away on the other side of the railway in what really *is* desert – mile upon mile of flat sandy or gritty ground without any sort of feature or fluctuation of contour. Here the tanks were in their element and as we roared across the plain, clouds of sand and dust blew up around us like some destroyer putting up a smoke screen.' Michael's Troop drove British Crusader cruisers, but some of the others had the new American General Stuarts, the light tanks always known as Honeys; Michael had them later.

'We fired our guns at the ranges, had a bite of lunch and set off home again on Jimmy's compass bearing, using our wirelesses, which came in very useful when two of us stopped for a few minutes in a sandstorm owing to petrol trouble. We were lucky to get home just as the sun was going down and as usual it was a beautiful sight.' The next day Michael went to the ranges by truck with Alex Barclay to watch a tank which had misfired previously. 'It's good fun going across that stuff in a tank but not the same in a truck.'

There was a lecture from the American who had developed the Honey, 'quite interesting with amusing episodes . . . He went on talking till it was quite dark, and the glow of cigarettes lit up the faces of the men.'

* *Shots in the Sand*, p. 70.

After another lecture – by a British officer returned from the fighting – Michael recorded with his usual optimism: 'Unfortunately I couldn't hear all of it but I don't think he said very much we didn't already know.'

Michael's scanty leisure, apart from a few hours' leave in Alexandria – on the day of Pearl Harbor and America's entry into the war – he filled mostly by writing. He tried to keep up his diary, and when issued with a strictly rationed air letter he squeezed in enough lines for three: his writing was clear but a magnifying glass was useful to read it. On 9 December he wrote: 'There's now always heaps to do. This is surely the most healthy way of things and I'd far rather have too much to do than too little. It means too that the days go quickly and one is always occupied, as are the men (a very good thing).

'When I wake up in the morning I can see through the opening in the tent the first pale streaks of day and if it is not too cold I enjoy shaving outside the tent with the sun just rising in the heavens. Of course it's always cold water, but we got used to that long ago! Usually most things are covered over with a layer of sand, especially if there's been a sandstorm the day before, and if one happens to be foolish enough to drop one's shaving stick, well – the sand'll have to come off first before use! These sandstorms, by the way, really consist of tiny particles of dust. We're getting used to them, of course, but they're not very pleasant and it gets into everything. In the Mess we turn the plates upside down before a meal starts so that the plates are clean when the food arrives!

'The food by the way is very good considering all things. It's amazing what you can do with Bully Beef. There are plenty of eggs, potatoes, vege's, oranges (hundreds of these; I wish I could send you some) and

Captain Tom Butler-Stoney, M.C., Royal Horse Artillery: Michael's great friend, later killed in action in 1943.

The badge of the Queen's Bays (The 2nd Dragoon Guards).

The Bays' first *khamsin* (sandstorm), 1942. Some of the drivers thought it was created by the Germans!

Brewing up, desert style.

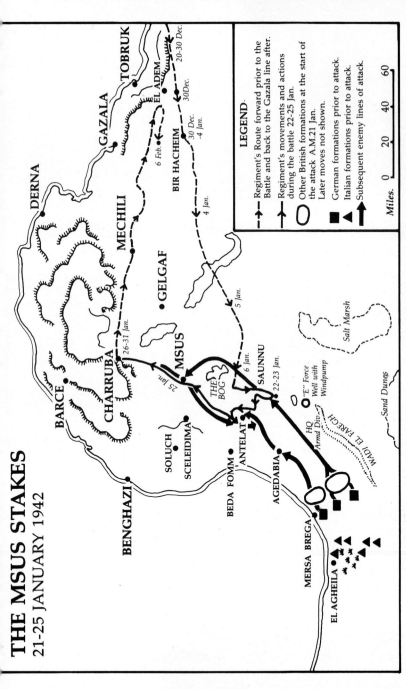

THE MSUS STAKES
21-25 JANUARY 1942

BENGHAZI
BARCE
DERNA
TOBRUK
GAZALA
MECHILI
CHARRUBA
GELGAF
MSUS
SOLUCH
SCELEIDIMA
BEDA FOMM
ANTELAT
AGEDABIA
MERSA BREGA
EL AGHEILA
SAUNNU
THE BOG
EL ADEM
BIR HACHEIM
Salt Marsh
Sand Dunes
WADI EL FAREGH
"E" Force
Well with
Windpump
HQ
Armd Div

20-30 Dec.
30 Dec.
30 Dec.
-4 Jan.
6 Feb.
4 Jan.
5 Jan.
26-31 Jan.
25 Jan.
6 Jan.
22-23 Jan.

LEGEND.
Regiment's Route forward prior to the
Battle and back to the Gazala line after.

Regiment's movements and actions
during the battle 22-25 Jan.

Other British formations at the start of
the attack A.M. 21 Jan.
Later moves not shown.

German formations prior to attack.

Italian formations prior to attack.

Subsequent enemy lines of attack.

Miles. 0   20   40   60

From *A History of The Queen's Bays, 1929–1945* by Major-General W.R. Beddington, CBE,
Warren & Son, Winchester, 1954.

Sermon on the Sand: Padre Morson at a Squadron service. Note Alex Barclay's band.

Holy Communion in the desert: the Padre with the Bays' medical unit.

Into Action: the Bays at the Battle of Gazala, taken from a tank as it advanced on the enemy.

our cooks make up all sorts of good dishes. I usually have my breakfast soon after 7 and we work from about 7.30 or 8 till 12, then lunch, work till tea at 4, quite often more work after tea. Then the washing operations, a sort of 'stand up bath' with the basin, although we can go over once a week to showers put up a mile or two away. I find I can keep pretty clean in cold water, and you can't call the sand dirty.

'We now have the great joy of reading newspapers and listening to the news on the wireless. We've got a set that can get the B.B.C. Overseas and it's very nice to hear some of the familiar voices of the announcers again. There's always a News about 8 p.m. which comes at the right time as we're finishing supper. We usually turn in early after censoring letters or writing our own. But I find no time for reading except for my Bible which I never miss if I can help it.'

He added, in one of the rare references to religion in letters to our parents, 'It gives me more comfort than anything else out here. What a pity many people don't get something out of it.'

On a Sunday at Amriya, 'we had Holy Communion in one of the Mess Tents,' he wrote in a letter to me: 'The attendance was only 4, but that doesn't matter. During the morning the Padre and I walked over to the Field Ambulance and we had a short informal service with the men there. The Padre is very good at that sort of thing; I thought he did it very well and I know the men enjoyed it. It is difficult in these days to put the real truth across to the men, but as long as they are continually reminded of Religion and what it means, that is the thing for the moment.' On the other Sunday the Squadron was out training early and had only a small and short service in the evening in the Mess Tent. Michael chatted afterwards with one of the men, 'whom I had wanted to talk to for a long time. He's a very nice fellow and a real Christian.'

Five days later, on 12 December the 1st Armoured Division under General Lumsden left their base camp for the battle zone far away in the west. Michael's Squadron went to the railway station the night before and loaded their tanks up a ramp on to flats, each barely wide enough for its tank, and spent the night in the train, starting early the next morning. Egyptian scenes were new enough to make the journey exciting; they passed a freight train carrying British tanks smashed by gun fire in the recent battles, and two hospital trains of wounded, mostly with long beards and staring eyes.

They went through a station with a name which then meant nothing: El Alamein.

At Mersa Matruh, the railhead, about two hundred miles east of the border of Italian Libya, now mostly in British hands again, they offloaded and waited a day and a night until all the Division was concentrated, ready to move.

Long afterwards Field Marshal Lord Alexander said that any division needed three months' training to be fit to fight in the desert, yet the Bays were expecting to be in action less than a month after landing. Michael commented: 'As long as we can get in a bit of training I don't mind how soon we go!'

He and his friends little knew what awaited them.

13

Before the Battle

When the Bays passed through the small gap in the Libyan frontier wire at noon, on 20 December 1941, in a sandstorm, the tide of the distant battle had turned completely. Rommel was in full retreat and the 1st Armoured Division had orders to join a turning movement south of Benghazi to cut the enemy off. The Bays hurried with all possible speed, which was slow enough considering the many hundreds of miles they must cover.

The strategic situation was less satisfactory than it looked. The Eighth Army lay dangerously strung out; supplies ran short; fresh troops expected from England were diverted to fight Japan; British naval losses had temporarily left the Mediterranean safe for Axis convoys and Rommel was about to be heavily reinforced. The 1st Armoured Division moved forward in ignorant bliss: Tom Butler-Stoney, acting adjutant of his gunner regiment and fresh from a visit to General Lumsden's headquarters, told Michael that 'the Division think Rommel has only got forty tanks left in Libya'.

It was a highly confident Regiment which had enjoyed the preliminary excitements and rigours of

desert travel before crossing the Libyan frontier. 'At
8 a.m. we sped off in formation,' Michael pencilled in
his diary, his ink having run out and ballpoint pens not
yet invented: 'We practised new signal procedures en
route and arrived in our new leaguer (or laager) around
3 o'clock in the afternoon. This time it was just a rocky
plain, with a cold Northerly wind blowing across. Once
again the tanks formed a circle turned outwards and
the men put up the tank covers for tents and each crew
made their little camp for the night.

'Then along came the lorries into the middle. Corporal Milton and his company unlimbered and a hot
meal was dealt out to a hungry Squadron.' While the
crews snuggled into their makeshift camps the officers
slept in the open 'with the stars as our ceiling, but a
furious wind beat across the plain and it was none too
warm.'

They had exercised for four days and were scattered
around the desert when orders came to join the chase
of Rommel at once. The orders were received at noon;
by two o'clock the Bays were on the move, with at least
two hundred miles to cover to the concentration area
south of Tobruk from which, it was believed, the 1st
Armoured Division would help finish Rommel for ever.
'All the travelling was done by day,' Michael recorded.
'Mile upon mile of waste land, covered occasionally
with patches of gorse and what looks like heather. It's
only the actual surface that changes – sometimes soft
sand, sometimes grit and dust, sometimes nothing but
rocks and stones, making the going extremely bad for
our vehicles. But they've stood up to it well and mine
are all complete.

'We used to halt at times through the day for a
meal which we cooked on our cookers from rations

which sometimes appeared and sometimes didn't. But we have a good little private supply of our own so we don't do badly.' Water was short; washing almost non-existent.

Each officer and his crew now slept under the tank cover rigged beside their tank, protected from freezing winds and grateful for every available blanket. 'We usually move just as it is getting light and often stop as the sun rises, for a quick breakfast . . . Corporal Coppen, Corporal Foster, and Lord are my crew and a very jolly party they are too. Lord is "Chief Steward" and looks after the rations, although most of us have a go at the cooking; they are better than me, I think!'

Foster was killed in 1942 and I failed to trace the others, but Michael's Troop was plainly a very happy one. The Squadron Quartermaster Sergeant, Bill Harvey, who became a police sergeant at Harwell Atomic Energy Establishment, recalled how Michael, 'mucked in with everything. Nothing was too much for him to do, he interested himself in everything. He was a chap who could get on with anybody. His tank crew thought a great deal of him at all times, a chap you could look up to and approach with any little question, no matter how small.'

Michael's crew even let him 'brew up' – make tea the desert way, which the Eighth Army had learned from the Australians. The taste and strength of the tea depended on the skill and timing with which the leaves, the condensed milk and the sugar were mixed into the water as it boiled in the open mess tin. The late Jimmy Dance MP said that 'Michael was one of the few officers in the Regiment who was allowed by his tank crew to brew tea, according to them a highly technical job. I was certainly never allowed to! They allowed me to get the water and the petrol, but as for the actual brewing I was never allowed to do this, and I always envied him his being given this great privilege.'

The tanks drove on across the desert, sixty or seventy miles a day. 'We saw plenty of signs of the Axis retreat,' Michael wrote. 'There were broken tanks, guns, vehicles, plenty of ammunition, bits of clothing, caps etc., as well as several odd papers and documents lying around' – and numerous shallow graves.

On Michael's twenty-second birthday, 21 December 1941, the Division's approach march was halted, owing to supply difficulties in the forward area, and the next ten days were spent in the desert thirty-five miles south-east of Tobruk. 'I have just come back from our Christmas morning service which was held in the open,' he wrote home, 'our Squadron band providing the music. We had all the familiar Christmas hymns and the Padre preached a short sermon. We had Holy Communion at 8 and this was rather chilly although very pleasant. The sun had only just risen and there was an icy cold wind.'

The Squadron Mess Tent was up again, used also as officers' dormitory at night, and the Mess corporal had discovered in a box the Christmas decorations used in England 'at dear old Greengates' the previous year. The Mess cook, Sergeant Brooks, had been chef of the Grand Hotel in Birmingham and 'he dishes up wonderful things, considering the circumstances'. He had numerous ways of serving the endless bully beef. 'Brooks got us up a wonderful Xmas dinner and I only wish the men could have had one as good although many of them rigged up some fair meals from what they'd got, and they enjoy cooking their own food rather than standing in a queue at the cook-house.' Nobody had luxuries; Colonel Draffen had sent an officer to scour Tobruk for Christmas extras for the men but other units had already swept the place.

Michael felt homesick during the hymn singing, as they all did. 'I thought of the family at home round the fire at Northaw and rather wished I was there too; but I don't regret these experiences we are having, and anyway it's all in the Great Plan.' Moreover, he actually received a letter on Christmas Day – not one of the many the family had been writing but from Hartley Holmes at Guildford, which had somehow jumped the hold-up in the Army Postal Unit.

The lack of family news was trying but 'we are making the most of things and everybody's pretty cheerful. We've certainly got some nice people with us and a lot of what we are doing is great fun.'

Orders came at last. The Eighth Army's assault on Rommel's defensive position had failed and another would not be mounted until the arrival of the 1st Armoured Division. The Bays drove onwards on 30 December, halted four days unexpectedly at Bir Hacheim, the water-hole which would be immortalised by the bravery of the Free French the next summer, and at last on 4 January 1942 began the dash which was expected to place them ready for the winning attack on the German line.

The Brigade moved, as the Regimental History records, in arrowhead formation, 'through strange and difficult country. There were sheer cliffs and deep dry *wadi* beds with thorn bushes four feet high and strange round conical hills rising straight out of the floor of the desert to a height of two hundred feet. All day much trouble was caused by large sharp boulders, which made the going very difficult for the wheeled vehicles in the transport echelons, cut the rubber tracks of the Honeys to pieces and caused damage to the oil lines of the Cruisers.'*

The Regiment leaguered at the appointed place and next morning resumed the march. But after crossing the ancient slave route they ran into an area littered with almost invisible little 'Thermos' bombs which had been dropped from the air to explode if crushed by a vehicle. Two tanks were blown up, without harm to their crews, and the Bays had to proceed for fifty miles in single file, creating such dust that crews often needed to stop and shovel their engine-covers clear. Several British-built Crusader cruisers, jammed by sand, had to be abandoned, though the American Honeys came through unscathed. The Bays stopped ten miles short and worked all night to service their remaining tanks, then reached their rendezvous near Saunnu on 7 January 1942, only to learn that Rommel had withdrawn to a yet more heavily fortified position at El Agheila, which the Eighth Army could not attack until stronger. The offensive was postponed again.

The Squadron leaguer proved more sheltered than any before, and even boasted a piece of grass. The Mess tent went up. Despite their gruelling march the crisp desert air kept them all 'extremely fit and well; it's really impossible not to be,' Michael commented. Their tanks, however, were not so fit and they spent the first day attempting to get them battle-worthy. Next day the Regiment started a tactical scheme but 'sandstorms

---

* A History of the Queen's Bays 1929–45, Warren & Son, Winchester, 1954, p. 34.

intervened and we returned after no more than an hour or two out. When the wind is up and the sand flying through the air conditions are rather unpleasant.'

Seven officers now shared the Squadron Mess and Michael's diary gives a glimpse of one of these last days before the battle: 'Peter Glynn captured a donkey yesterday which he found in a herd miles from anywhere and he's now gone out to try and swap it for a sheep, or two, to feed the Squadron on. Gordon and Chris have gone off to fetch water from a neighbouring *bir* and see if they can pot at something with a shotgun. Peter Gill banged up his head on the lid of our M.3 this morning and is now recuperating on his bed. I've been writing some Airgraphs . . .'

Another officer had driven off north-west, by compass across the desert, to obtain Regimental canteen stores from Benghazi. He was a long time away, and reported to Colonel Draffen on return that it was eighty miles there but a hundred and fifty back – he had got on a wrong bearing and missed the leaguer! His supplies – Italian tins of vegetables, sardines, jam, condensed milk and cigarettes – were as welcome as Peter Glynn's sheep which gave mutton for stew for the whole Squadron, with liver for the Officers' Mess, 'the tenderest I have tasted for a long time,' Michael wrote home: 'There's always plenty of something to eat, anyway. Water is a problem but sometimes we hit upon a well and so add to things. At this time of year, of course, we don't get especially thirsty, but the more water we get the more washes we can get! Actually it doesn't seem at all uncomfortable to go 2 or 3 days without a wash nowadays!

'We brought the Squadron Band out here with us and when we are stopping at places like this, it comes in most useful and popular, as you can imagine.'

The Bays and all the 2nd Armoured Brigade remained anchored to this bit of desert. The unwelcome delay was compounded by other adverse factors. Many tanks were still under repair; training with the rest had been stopped by petrol rationing after storms cut the sea supply route to Benghazi. And the 1st Armoured Division was a brigade short since one of its three brigades had arrived in North Africa by an earlier convoy and had been thrown into the battle already. Then came another blow: the popular Divisional Commander, Major-General Herbert Lumsden, had been wounded in an air raid when visiting the forward area. His temporary substitute was not a cavalryman; his instincts and training did not make for a smooth command (during one inspection Lumsden had looked hard at Michael, asked his name afterwards and then said: 'I last saw him in his nursery!').

Colonel Draffen reorganised his tanks, giving each Squadron one Troop of Honeys. In 'A' Squadron Alex Barclay chose Michael to command it: he and his men handed over their British Crusaders and moved into the lighter and very reliable American Honeys, excellent for reconnaissance. A few days later, over the protests of the commanding officers, the Divisional Support Group was taken away; thus the gunners and motorised infantry who had trained with the tanks, so that each regiment knew its supporting units as well-tried friends, were torn from them and sent to the front to relieve a Support Group which had been in action for seven weeks. The Brigade could not train properly with the replacements because of the shortage of petrol.

Everyone, however, believed that Rommel was at his

last gasp. After returning from a Squadron briefing on 8 January Michael wrote in his diary: 'Rommel has got some good positions near El Agheila, but once we are organised it shouldn't take much to push him out.' No one knew that Rommel's Intelligence had informed him that the 1st Armoured Division were without desert battle experience and that their untried Support Group had been sent forward to face him. He was more than ever determined to strike back as soon as he could.

14

Defeat at Msus

'There's rather a lazy atmosphere about at present,' Michael noted, though routine kept everyone busy. Alex Barclay's band played in the evenings. Michael had appointed himself Squadron Editor: 'I copy down the news from the wireless, make out a short news sheet and pin it up so that the Squadron can learn what's going on.' The subalterns organised a night march competition between each Troop and in a typical cavalry gesture cooked a meal themselves to serve as prize to the winning team.

The Mess tent was again a dormitory but Michael preferred to sleep beside his tank crew – 'There's really more room down there, I can get to bed when I like and there is always a chance for a Quiet Time at night as they like going to sleep early.' Michael had a pocket New Testament with a zip fastener to keep out the sand. He also had *Daily Light*, the famous book of brief meditations for morning and evening, all in words from the Bible, which had been compiled in the late eighteenth century by the Bagster family: though despised by some as the lazy Christian's pick-me-up, *Daily Light* has been invaluable to men and women whose duties prevent or delay unhurried devotions. 'Think of me in my bivouac at night,' Michael wrote to me on 8 January 1942, 'with my "Daily Light" and N.T. He keeps me wonderfully alive and ready for anything. It's wonderful to think one has complete protection from the Lord.'

Nothing could happen out of the Lord's control, who had abolished death in any sense that mattered; *'To live is Christ; to die is gain,'* Michael had pencilled in capitals above St Paul's epistle to the Philippians, where the verse is found (chapter 1, verse 21).

Before dawn on 22 January Michael and the others were woken with the message that the Regiment would move in an hour. German and Italian troops had advanced from the El Agheila line which the British had been preparing to attack, 'and we were going to meet them'.

Colonel Draffen motored off to the Brigadier's Orders conference. Afterwards he had to trudge back on foot the last half-mile to the leaguer because his scout car broke down. This aggravating delay was the prelude to a battle in which bravery and professional skill were to be at the mercy of untoward events compounded by strategic errors of the higher command.

'We were hardly in luck to start with,' Michael recorded, 'as some of the tanks were non-runners and the net result was that "A" Squadron started with only two Troops and these not complete ones.' The Regiment arrived nearly thirty minutes late at the start line but others were later and the Brigade did not move until 11 a.m. In about an hour they passed Saunnu, written large on battle maps but merely a well with a windpump. A few miles south they were halted for an hour, wondering why.

The Colonel returned from another Brigade conference with news that enemy tanks, previously assumed
to be conducting nothing but a 'reconnaissance in
force', were pouring through Agedabia, only twenty
miles away to the south-west, having overrun or outmanoeuvred the British forward troops. These were all
under the command of 1st Armoured Division, whose
piecemeal defeat had already begun, though Michael
and other junior officers neither knew nor would have
believed it.

The Regiment changed direction west and about
5 p.m. reached another rendezvous, only to learn that an
enemy column was now north-west of them, cutting off
the Brigade from the British forward base at Benghazi.
The Bays turned once again, 'learning the news that
some tanks (thought to be Italian) were a few miles
away', and soon leaguered for the night: at that period
in the Desert War the opposing forces seldom fought
after dark.

'The next morning (23 January) we were away early
and were given the alarming news that an enemy
column had attacked our "B" Echelon during the
night at Saunnu.' (The Brigade 'B' Echelon were the
'soft' vehicles carrying workshops, stores etc. – and
Ermyntrude. 'A' Echelon were the ammunition and
petrol lorries.) While the other units in the Brigade
hurried west to block an enemy attack on the army's
vital supply line, the Bays, with one battery of guns,
went to rescue the Echelon.

They started south towards Saunnu in arrowhead
formation, Michael's Squadron under Alex Barclay in
the van, through the thickest fog they had ever met
in the desert. Until the fog lifted an hour later Michael
could see only his own tanks, the Squadron Leader's

being nothing but a rumble. According to current tactical theory Colonel Draffen should have been able to see all his armour but he too was virtually fogbound, and his tank soon broke down. He had to transfer, and leave his tank crew behind, and never saw them again, nor the Regimental Headquarters fitters, all of whom were made prisoners.

Michael 'found "B" Echelon to be quite all right although they'd had plenty of excitements during the night and taken several prisoners.' The news that thirty Italians were in the bag sent morale soaring; but the battle was already going against the 2nd Armoured Brigade. 'We paused for a bit,' Michael continues, 'and then proceeded, joining up with the Brigade on a bit of higher ground. A lot of firing then started and Gordon's Troop were fired on by A/T guns and his tank shed a track and had to be abandoned.' The noise, and the mushroom plumes of black smoke in the distance where tanks or petrol dumps exploded, were novelties to the Bays that day – a baptism of fire for Michael and all in the Squadron who had not fought in France.

Msus was an untidy battle with people frequently facing the wrong way through no fault of their own. 'We saw what we found out afterwards to be the 10th Hussars making a spectacular charge in the opposite direction to us, and the firing increased. The 10th were definitely badly trapped and suffered casualties but they must have hit the enemy up all right.' The enemy could afford the loss but the 10th Hussars dropped to eight tanks; of the entire Brigade, only the Bays remained comparatively strong, although several of their tanks were no longer serviceable.

At about one o'clock the Brigade moved north-east, with the Bays as Headquarters' advanced guard, but after an hour received orders to change direction again and drove (the words 'advance' or 'retreat' were meaningless) for another two and a half hours.

At about 4.30 p.m. they reached the north–south track between Antelat and Msus airfield, which lay some thirty miles north. They wheeled and took up position astride the track, facing south-west.

'We saw a whole lot of vehicles on a hill to our left,' Michael records. 'There seemed to be no movement of any kind and we thought they must be our own. We soon found we were wrong when guns opened fire on "C" Squadron who were leading.' The Colonel sent 'A' Squadron to reconnoitre. Alex Barclay had only six tanks left, and Michael's was the one Troop still functioning in name.

'We took up positions observing this hill and we refilled from a petrol lorry which dashed from tank to tank.' They believed that enemy forces on the hill 'were very small and sooner or later we'd just surround them or shell them out. Alex suggested we should "brew up".' Just as Michael and his men were enjoying hot peas and bully and a mug of tea, the enemy sallied out in strength, guns blazing. Michael's tea was too hot to drink and had to be thrown away. 'There's still time for a laugh,' was his comment on this unceremonious end to dinner as they retired in haste, having been ordered not to engage.

They rejoined the Regiment at sunset. That night, absurdly, an enormous batch of letters arrived. Michael received nearly twenty which family and friends had been writing before, during and since his voyage. But being dog-tired and duty officer, he had no time for reading – 'Still, they are safe in my pocket.' It was a week before he had read the lot.

In the middle of the night the leaguer moved five miles, 'presumably to put the Germans off the scent'. At dawn the squadrons resumed observation positions. 'We had pot shots at a large German gun and a couple of tanks (the former was captured by "C" Squadron later), took a German prisoner (driving one of our trucks full of food) and rescued a scout car and crew captured by the enemy.' The Germans made no serious move anywhere: Eighth Army headquarters optimistically and inaccurately told the world that Rommel's offensive had been contained.

Action was spasmodic – a day of shelling and being shelled. 'We didn't have much time to feel bored, with the woomp woomp of the shells all around us,' Michael wrote to me later, 'and the patter of machine guns. Of course we heard our own too and didn't they sound nice. It was a great sight too to see our guns in action – a little sheet of flame, then a threatening bang, a pause and then clouds of smoke around the enemy's positions, and one strains one's eyes to see the results. You can see a long way in the desert on good days and most days are good days out here. Vehicles when moving at speed send up little clouds of dust and tanks look very like destroyers at sea with the spray of their wash floating back behind. Then if they turn you lose them in a cloud of this dust which is as good as any smoke screen. We could see some of the German tanks and guns quite clearly through our glasses when they were still 2 or 3 miles away and of course much of this ground is very flat which makes things easier.'

The desert fighting at this stage of the campaign had almost an air of manoeuvres – lethal, but not sordid. No civilians or homesteads were around: the few Bedouin could be guided away before a battle. The desert mercifully lacked the misery and foulness of war in populated parts where the helpless and the children are caught in destruction and fear. The opposing armies were fighting it out on their own, the last 'professional' campaign in history with something of the chivalry of some earlier wars.

But no sensitive man, however professional, could quite forget that his actions must maim or kill. A senior officer has written: 'Michael was kindness itself and would never have done a bad turn to anyone, let alone being involved in destroying God's creation except as it was part of the duty which he loyally accepted.'

He added: 'His strength was kindness exemplified and that rare quality, emphasised by all religious leaders: composure.' Gordon Anthony said: 'If Michael was worried, he didn't show it; he must have bottled it up inside him.'

Michael put it differently: 'Psalm 91 was certainly the lesson of the day with the shells falling all around.' Michael knew that psalm well: 'He that dwelleth in the secret place of the most High shall abide under the shadow of the Almighty. I will say the Lord, He is my refuge and my fortress: my God; in him will I trust.'

Next day, the fateful 25 January 1942, completed the defeat of the 1st Armoured Division. They had been unable to call up air support because aviation fuel was so scarce in the forward areas that the RAF (and, fortunately, the Luftwaffe) were almost grounded.

At daylight Michael was ordered to take his own Honey tank and Corporal Findlay's to join a small composite column composed of field guns, anti-tank guns and a rifle company, and known as Pomphrey Force after its commander, 'a charming major in

the Northumberland Yeomanry, who wore a large
Australian type hat and dashed about in a 15 cwt truck.'
Brigade ordered Pomphrey Force to enter Antelat from
the north, 'but no sooner had we opened out fanwise
than the Germans opened fire from their hill, and
several columns were seen to be moving.'

About 7 a.m. Pomphrey sent Michael to reconnoitre
some German Anti-Tank guns on the right. He raced
off under cover of a ridge and as he topped it the
Germans saw him. 'They and we opened fire almost
simultaneously. A shell hit the top of my driver's flap
and broke the hinge, penetrating deeply.'

They were all shaken but the driver, Corporal
Coppen, was unhurt. Trooper Lord, the gunner, was
certain they had hit the German but it was a narrow
escape: Michael's tank must have been at a range or
angle which just prevented the shell causing a sham-
bles, for on that day the Bays made the unwelcome
discovery that German 88 mm shells could penetrate
the British armour-plate. Peter Glynn was killed a few
hours later when a shell passed right through him and
out again on the far side of his turret. But British shells
often merely bounced off German armour-plate.

Colonel Draffen heard the guns and saw a powerful
German column nearing Pomphrey's right flank. He
ordered 'C' Squadron to help, but no sooner had its
counter-attack started than Brigade made the whole
regimental group retire. It was too late to counter-
mand the Squadron attack, which went in gallantly
with casualties on both sides. Michael then observed
the rest of the Regiment in retreat. 'Later, we could
see German tanks going forward on the left, and
Pomphrey decided to withdraw to stop being cut off
between the two. The firing and explosions were pretty

loud on the left as we started back but we weren't hindered.'

By now, in the words of the Regimental History, 'There were literally hundreds of vehicles of all descriptions streaming back in confusion along, and on each side of, the Antelat–Msus track.' As one Bays officer recalled: 'It would be fair to describe the withdrawal, at some stages, as being at an extended gallop!' The battle was aptly named afterwards, in racing jargon, the Msus Stakes.

But the German eye-witness, Colonel Von Mellenthin, who claimed that 'the British fled madly over the desert in one of the most extraordinary routs of the war,' was wrong; for though outgunned and outmanoeuvred the 2nd Armoured Brigade – or what was left of it – had not lost their courage. Colonel Draffen organised the Bays in three columns and the Regimental History describes how 'Amid the welter of confusion each of the three columns did its utmost to fight an orderly retreat, each of them taking up first one position and then another on any feature that offered itself.'* It was a most difficult action for the Colonel. 'I'm told he fought magnificently,' wrote Michael, 'and was one of the last to leave the battlefield.'

Pomphrey Force had no tanks except Michael's two American Honeys (one being damaged) and could not fight rearguard actions. 'We did a good number of miles without stopping,' Michael records, 'and whilst our A/T guns took up positions on a hill we refilled our two tanks from one of several dumps which a small party of R.E. or R.A.S.C. were setting alight to prevent them falling into German hands.' While

---

* *op. cit.*, p. 48

refuelling Michael saw German tanks coming up on his left. The British guns were scoring hits on them but he was uncomfortably aware that shells from these German tanks might blow up the fuel dump and him with it. As soon as Michael had finished refuelling, Pomphrey ordered the column to continue the withdrawal – or rout – making a 'smoke screen' of sand as lorries, gun carriers and tanks sped north.

Scattered groups closed haphazardly. Communications had broken down: Michael could make no wireless contact with Alex Barclay, and Barclay's tank was in fact already a wreck and he was leading his crew on foot with the enemy all around. He rejoined three days later after an adventurous escape.

Michael heard Gordon Anthony on the air, saying that he was with the 9th Lancers; and Squadron-Sergeant-Major Ayling, saying that he was cut off. West of Msus airfield, already in enemy hands, Pomphrey and Michael met several Bays officers with their tanks, 'and the Doc in his scout car as alive as ever'.

The officers dismounted from their vehicles to discuss the next move. They decided to join up with Brigade Headquarters somewhere farther north. 'We spent a little too long over the map and got shelled by A/T guns who turned us nicely into about 15 German tanks coming at top speed towards us.'

In this alarming crisis the slightest panic might be disastrous. However, Michael recorded laconically in the diary, 'The whole force shook clear of them and later we ran into a patrol of the 11th Hussars who gave us the petrol we needed so badly. From then onwards the day was uneventful.' Indeed so, for Rommel had cunningly deceived Eighth Army Command into ordering 2nd Armoured Brigade away from the vital battle

instead of towards it, thus ensuring his recapture of
Benghazi. The day ended lamely thirty-five miles north
of Msus at Charruba, where Michael found Divisional
and Brigade Headquarters leaguered with the remnants
of all the Regiments involved in the Msus Stakes,
together with 'plenty of columns of various sorts, and
the Guards':

'As I lay down in my desert bed once again it was
hard to realise the amazing events that had happened
in the last 24 hours. The day went by without any idea
of time, not much of place and certainly very little of
exactly how far the Germans had succeeded in getting.
Sometimes things were very amusing, sometimes interesting, sometimes rather alarming. We were pretty tired
by the time it had all finished, and a bit bewildered, I
suppose.'

In letters home he could only give a guarded reference to 'hectic days'. To our parents he wrote: 'Things
happen so quickly out here that you don't get much
time for thinking. You do all the thinking after it's
all over and you're lying by your tank looking up at
the stars and just dropping off to sleep. Then you
remember all the queer experiences you've had and
thank God for protecting you all this time. He certainly
gave me a *lot* of protection and I shan't forget it.'

Michael and his crew had been under frequent shell
fire, had attacked the enemy and turned tight corners.
By chance of war they had not seen men dying before
their eyes at close range or heard the screams of men
trapped in a burning tank. The 10th Hussars had
suffered badly but the Bays' casualties were mercifully
light: one officer, two non-commissioned officers and
two troopers killed, and some five or six of their support
troops. Nearly a year later, when the Bays were back on

the Msus battlefield after the victory of Alamein and the final advance, they found that the Germans had not removed either the damaged tanks or the bodies. The Colonel asked the Padre to take a subaltern, a sergeant and some troopers to give Christian burials. To their amazement those bodies which had not been burnt 'clean' were in almost perfect preservation. Peter Glynn's features were still recognisable, so dry was the atmosphere. 'I found it altogether very moving,' wrote Padre Morson fifty years after the battle, 'and those with me were most helpful and co-operative.' Burying these bodies 'was much less ghastly than dealing with those recently killed in battle.'

Michael's first action was over. Some days later he wrote to me: 'I keep thinking, whilst we are having a comparatively quiet time, of all the things I ought to have done during the battle to win the war quicker! But it's rather stupid starting to think like that, although one can of course learn a lesson from every little movement right or wrong out here. Anyway, we gave them a good crack.

'But it does come back to me again and again how wonderful it is to have a Friend in whom one can put one's trust. Those verses in Psalm 91 about the arrows flying about you are really a wonderful promise, and I do realise how much I have to thank God "Who is with thee, whithersoever thou goest."'

15

The Troop

When Jackie Harman, the future general, rejoined the Regiment from Divisional Headquarters after the Battle of Msus, to be second in command of 'A' Squadron, and later Squadron Leader, he found that 'Michael's bravery was current talk by both officers and men. To me it was evident by the calm and composed way he viewed the prospect of the fighting that was to come that popular opinion was right. It was often the quiet and diffident – which Michael was – that were the really brave, while the extrovert was less anxious to risk his life.'

His brother officer Peter Willett made the same point when discussing Michael's '. . . very happy relationship with his Troop. He was not, of course, the kind of leader, popularised by war literature, who leaps on to the parapet brandishing a sword and shouting "On, men!" Soldieers, so far as their collective responses were concerned, are very complex and unpredictable. The only rule I have been able to discern is that they see through bombast and heroic posturing with an unerring eye, and have a corresponding appreciation of what is genuine. The relationship of a tank commander and troop leader with his crews is very close, and its success must be based on mutual trust and affection as much as positive leadership of the kind glamourised in military fiction.'

One night in the desert the officers of 'A' Company were chatting on this subject. Michael was writing, with only one ear on the conversation, when one of them cited him as an example of the truth that the diffident man is braver than the extrovert. One of his best friends replied jokingly: 'Michael's not brave – he is merely too deaf to hear what's going on!' Michael turned and smiled.

Immediately after the rearguard action which was so nearly a rout, the remnants of the three regiments of 2nd Armoured Brigade had been temporarily reformed as a composite unit and Michael went to a squadron made up of 10th Hussars and Bays. His own tank, considered unbattleworthy, was lent with its crew to the 9th Lancers as a Forward Observation Post and Michael changed to another. One of his new crew, Trooper Edward Parrish, remembered long afterwards how Michael 'carried a small and rather worn Bible which he read as another would read a novel'.

Though they went on patrol the enemy was not sighted again. British strategy had been ruined by Rommel's audacious advance, and by early February 1942 the Eighth Army was back within thirty miles of Tobruk in a series of positions or 'boxes' guarded by minefields: the Gazala Line. The Queen's Bays was reformed and re-equipped. Alex Barclay, having rejoined unscathed, to the delight of Ermyntrude who had been under fire herself, became second in command of the Regiment, and Jimmy Dance took over 'A' Squadron.

'We have gone back for a time,' Michael wrote home

on 9 February, 'but are strengthening our muscles for the biggest blow the Germans ever had and this will silence them!!'

Life fell into a routine of watching, training and patrols. No man's land was a great stretch of desert where it was possible to penetrate as much as eighty miles without sighting the enemy. Michael loved 'riding in a tank at top speed, through the coolness of a desert morning, the sun only just up, the moisture only beginning to dry on the ground.' Sometimes the forays were less armoured and offensive: 'I've been out "water hunting" this afternoon. We get a daily ration of water regularly but although this is ample for drinking at present, the more water we can get the better. Therefore every so often we go out with cans in a truck and search the various *birs* (wells). I wasn't so successful this afternoon and came back empty. Actually it didn't seem quite the right day to go as it was pouring with rain! But I expect tomorrow the *birs* will be full and we shall have more success. There was a strong wind all today which changed for no reason in the afternoon from East to West but the wind often does that.'

The weather was still cool enough to sunbathe leaning against a tank. The heavy rain of late February clothed the desert with grass and brought out the spring flowers. Hundreds of tiny pale blue crocuses, mixed with other flowers, yellow and red, spread like a Persian carpet around the Squadron Mess tent. Michael made it his job to keep the Mess supplied with flowers. Wherever the Troop drove, these flowers 'whose names I know not, gave me immense pleasure to see. There are plenty of varieties if you look for them. People moan about the aridness and bleakness of the desert but there is plenty of His work to behold if you *want* to behold it. Unfortunately not many people do.'

Apart from occasional air raids the Regiment's chief enemy was boredom. They had no amenities except what they could improvise. The combination of dis-comfort – 'a real tinker's life' – with inaction was a stiff test for Troop leaders, who had no aids to the maintenance of morale except their own resourceful-ness. Inter-Troop and inter-Squadron football matches were arranged; Michael resumed his Squadron welfare post and organised debates and news bulletins for the notice board.

He was never happier than when alone with his Troop. 'We've just been out on a scheme (all day),' he wrote home. 'The scheme was quite interesting but very dusty as it usually is when you have a lot of vehicles travelling together in the same direction. Going out, the wind was behind us which means that you get your own dust in your face, but with goggles, of course, it doesn't matter so much. Coming back we had the wind blowing straight at us so that all your dust blows away behind. In the middle of the scheme we had our usual "brew-up" – a good mug of tea and a bit of eats – which is always something to look forward to.'

Helping his crew to 'brew up' was always 'good fun'. Michael wrote in another letter: 'We've just been "brewing up" (ie cooking our dinner) which consisted of a tin of bully, a tin of someone's "steak and vegetables", some tinned peas (Italian) and ground up biscuits. All this heated in a home made frying pan on a fire of petrol, wood and these little twigs which you find all over the desert – obviously put here for our use, as they're always bone dry and just right for our fires.'

Tea continued to loom large in their lives: 'All cups

(or mugs) of tea are good out here but they differ in taste according to the water. In England, of course, all water seems to taste the same, but out here there are all sorts of different varieties and it becomes quite a topic of conversation. We get a normal issue of half a gallon per day but above that we can usually fill cans and small tanks from the local wells, and that's how we manage to get a good wash.

'We haven't got our Mess Tent up at present and so we live with our crews which is good fun. They always make superb mugs of tea which I enjoy, and Bully and Biscuit still seems to taste good. (Ah! My gunner has just suggested boiling up some tea. A very good suggestion!) The canteen came back yesterday after refilling and each tank's crew made its own small purchases. We get a lot of stuff that came from Australia, New Zealand, and are still getting Singapore's products. One of the most popular is tinned pineapple and other tinned fruit. Not particularly expensive. There always seems to be plenty of chocolate to buy too, and the men can get plenty of cigarettes. We all get a free issue of cigarettes and matches out here, but as I don't smoke I keep mine as a sort of reserve for my crew in case they run out. My packets always seem to come in useful. I keep the matches for myself as they can always come in handy. We also get an issue of Rum every so often. We have ours in the Mess mixed with odd things and its very enjoyable served hot in the evenings. I only like it if it's very weak, and then it just warms you up. I expect it's good for me!'*

Jackie Harman found that 'Michael had a deep sense

---

* But it was no use keeping a little rum in the mug for the cold mornings: the atmosphere was so dry that Michael Halsted discovered that his rum had evaporated overnight! (*Shots in the Sand*, p. 211)

of compassion and took endless pains on behalf of his
men by whom he was particularly well liked. I remember him standing up to me on behalf of one of his
men whom I had criticised as being a fairly worthless
individual. I think I was right in my assessment but he
was even more right in befriending one of his men.'
These men were a mixed enough bag, for in addition to
pre-war regulars, the troopers of 'A' Squadron included
a Durham coal-miner, a dock labourer who had done
several stretches in prison and a student who was
afterwards a university lecturer. Michael got along with
them all.

When nothing was doing he retreated to his tiny
one-man 'bivvy' tent. The faithful Selby had dug out
the sand to a depth of four feet, and 'put my "bivvy'
over the top. There is now therefore room for my
camp bed which I haven't slept in since Christmas.
I shall certainly sleep a good night tonight. He has
dug sort of ledges into the side, making shelves where
I can put things. Altogether very snug.' Sitting outside
on his canvas chair, or on the camp bed, Michael
wrote letters or read Trollope. My mother had posted
a parcel of Barchester novels to amuse him on the
voyage, and like all the mail it reached him in the
desert. Trollope deservedly had a come-back during
the war; few books were more soothing for exiles from
an England which, socially, was still not so very far
from Trollope's. James Dance, writing some twenty-six
years later, could remember quite clearly Michael's love
for Trollope. My mother had also sent a book about
cricket which Michael enjoyed and passed round the
Squadron's cricketers, including the Post Corporal who
was their wicket-keeper and a sergeant who was their
fast bowler. 'They're a grand lot.'

The Squadron Mess Tent had also been dug into the sand, making it cooler. The Mess sergeant had made the tent 'look extremely nice and pleasant' and unlike some Squadrons they had a wireless set, which could be tuned to 'a variety of stations, but I like it most for the fact that we can get the News, as there isn't much time for listening to music. But I've got a friend who isn't in my Squadron but is often over here who knows almost every bit of music written, if you know what I mean, and always finds something good on our wireless when he visits us.'

They had a 'very jolly little Mess (six of us)' but Michael preferred his bivvy unless it was too cold. Harman recalled: 'He was quiet, self-contained and always cheerful. He lived a rather withdrawn life although I do not feel that he was in any way unhappy. He just did not participate in some of the pursuits of young officers in a Cavalry Regiment in wartime when off duty. This does not mean that he was dull or priggish; certainly no-one thought any the worse of him for this. Living the narrow and confined lives that we did I think we all welcomed differences in outlook, interests and character.'

He never became close to any of the Squadron officers but one of his dearest friends was nearby, for Tom Butler-Stoney's battery had been returned to the Brigade and attached to the Bays. Tom wrote early in March that Michael was 'looking most extraordinarily fit and well'.

'I'm writing this sitting on an empty shell box by my tank in the shade,' Michael wrote early in April 1942: 'It's a hot day but as is usual nowadays there's a nice strong breeze and this keeps us cool. The sun gets up earlier now, of course, and one of the best times of the day is from about 6.45 to 9 when it is coolish and fresh and very often quite a dew on the ground. Then there is the hot period of the day and then later in the evening it once more gets cool. The nights are often quite warm.' The flowers were still around, and '. . . plenty of birds about, although you don't see many during the day, and often if you can listen, a regular concert is going on. Sometimes during the day they'll come quite close to you and eject a piercing whistle. They often follow a tank too and alight quite close when we halt. But still I do miss the cheerful songs of the English birds that we used to hear so much at Marlborough and long to hear them again, although of course it's the same for everyone!'

Michael loved the early mornings. He had a small hymn book, and 'the first hymn of all is grand for a fine sunny morning, and I often read it first thing: "When morning gilds the skies; my heart awakening cries, May Jesus Christ be praised." Do you remember the tune we had at Charterhouse to it?* That one that goes running up the scale, as if it was accompanying the red sun as it slowly rises: what a hymn to put joy into your heart, to fill you with that delightful freshness that we should all have in the morning! Then there is my "Daily Light" which was in my breast pocket all through our last battle, and which although slightly sandy and dusty is as complete as ever.'

Sundays were too often like other days, either because of patrols or exercises or because of the 'blinding

---

* 'Laudes Domini' by Sir Joseph Barnby, 1838–96.

sandstorms' which now afflicted them, ruining any work outside: 'The sand gets in anywhere and everywhere and pours itself over the table, the cups and saucers and the food . . . I'd love to find out why the wind blows non-stop for 2 days from South to North and brings up all the sand and dust from the Sahara, and then at midday yesterday it changed and blew from North to South carting all the sand and dust back again. Of course we much prefer the N wind as it is cooler.' The *Khamsin* winds were a time when they might all 'get very dispirited if not on our guard! The best plan is always to keep *cheerful!*'

One Sunday when no patrols were ordered, and no wind blew, a most beautiful day, they had a Squadron church parade in the morning 'which was extremely pleasant and comforting'. The band played for the hymns: 'Earlier we had had Holy Communion at 8. Talking of church services, we've had some in very queer places and our methods have often been very funny, but what does it matter? The Padre is an expert at improvising and sometimes he has the back of a lorry for the altar and other times nothing at all. But I think you will agree that these are minor details in a place like this. Lately things have been fairly normal and we have had our "mobile" altar, which shuts up and is made of very nice mahogany. It was specially made for the Regiment when we were in Surrey.'

The Squadrons were spread over a wide area and Padre Morson, who had gained a high reputation in the Msus battle, was temporarily responsible for two other regiments also. One Sunday when he could not get over to 'A' Squadron he invited Michael to take a short voluntary service, 'the first time I've ever done it'.

'The Padre lent me some of his books and we had

a chap play a concertina for the music of the hymns. There were about ten of us altogether. I read the bit about "Seek ye first the Kingdom of God, and all these things shall be added to you." We ended with "The Day Thou Gavest", which is always a favourite hymn with the troops.

'They said afterwards that they liked it very much and could it be repeated? One chap in particular – a wireless operator whose father died recently, an awfully nice chap – told me he really appreciated it.' This may have been the former Bays trooper who wrote long afterwards about Michael: 'It takes quite a lot of courage to so openly declare one's Faith, when Religion was looked on a little sideways by the majority of the rank and file. Tell a man serving overseas that his family and his home has been wiped out by an enemy bomb and then expect his Faith to remain unshaken is asking a lot.'

Army padres work under the disadvantage of being regarded primarily as officers, not ministers, and however devoted to their vocation they come into the men's lives from outside. A Troop officer inevitably knows his men better. Michael accepted the spiritual responsibility. As Peter Willett commented: 'The large majority of soldiers were indifferent to formal religious observance and were unwilling attenders of church parades, but they would have respect and affection for someone like Michael whose faith was patently sincere, simple, even ingenuous.' The Padre greatly welcomed Michael's help. 'He used to take short informal services for his Squadron on Sunday evenings,' Basil Morson wrote afterwards to my parents, 'and the men have often told me how much they appreciated them . . . Michael was of us all the most devout and real sincere Christian and I have known what his religion meant to him, that it was the dominant factor in his life and we all admired him for it.'

Michael used to pass round religious books and papers among his men but he did not find it easy to say anything positive to help them towards faith; he knew that example was not enough yet felt that blunt or repeated attempts to win them for Christ might repel. He never resolved the dilemma. The very depths of his own feelings inhibited him. 'I often think these days,' he wrote to me on 2 April, 'that I'm not doing enough for everybody, or (more important) enough for God. But I feel this is a healthy state of mind. One cannot tell how short or long one's life will be; therefore we should all be going flat out. "Redeem the time" was the Apostle's advice, wasn't it? I must try to obey.'

That same letter of 2 April reveals again his conviction that he and I would never see each other for the last time: 'Well, John,' he wrote, 'I'm still in the finest health and wonderfully happy out here, although looking forward more and more to the happy day we shall meet again, whichever side it is. We now get up rather earlier than usual, but it works out so that I have a much longer time before breakfast for a nice Quiet Time in my tent. I expect you can guess what a difference it makes to my work, my thoughts, my conversation and my every action. Things do sometimes seem wrong and sometimes I do feel a little despondent; but always when I can have a time in my tent in the morning – just alone with the Lord – then everything falls into its proper place, difficulties work themselves out and all seems for the best.'

He reverted to this theme in another letter on 29 April: 'The best time of all was about a fortnight ago when we got up very early for about half an hour and then had about one and a half hours before breakfast. Most people seemed to like going to sleep again, but I sprang on the time for the "Quiet Hour" which we all need so much. It is a wonderful place, the desert, in many ways. The stillness is something you cannot get in England now and it was wonderful to have "that perfect peace which the world cannot give". Now we've put the clocks on and so do not get quite so much time in the morning. Still I take every available minute and it's amazing how reviving it is after a hard or dusty day to slip into my bivvy and as somebody says, "the dust and heat can be washed away by His blood."

'I still have plenty of difficulties but all have their answer through Him. Please pray that I *never* forget what He has done for me. Often things will go very well and I am liable to forget what I owe Him unless I am always vigilant. Sometimes I find it hard to decide on my attitude to various things said or done here and there, but if each time I take the problem to Him, I know I shall get an answer.'

One of the 'difficulties' – which he did not mention – was his increasing deafness.

Though he was at a peak of physical fitness, the noise and tensions of the Msus battle had undoubtedly affected his hearing because the inherited defect was a nerve deafness. Knowing that another big battle was brewing, he did everything he could to cover up, lest he be parted from his men. His attempts to disguise his deafness made him seem slow in the uptake. A partially deaf person suffers a slight pause before spoken words sort themselves out; he may also miss one or two words in a sentence and is especially at a disadvantage if the subject suddenly changes. A quick intellect will often guess the meaning correctly without hearing the whole sentence; Michael was not quick, though very intelligent. Like most deaf people he preferred to pretend not to understand, and to seek further explanation, when in fact he had not heard.

The Colonel and Michael's Squadron Leader were worried, both for Michael's sake and his men's. It was not so much that in his tank during battle he might mishear an order, for this would be received through the wireless operator whose voice would be clear and familiar. But at vital conferences or appreciations before action he might lose an essential sentence or, worse, might leave under the genuine impression that he had heard words which were not precisely those which had been spoken. In a battle the slightest misunderstanding may make the difference between life and death, success and defeat.

There were other hazards. One night (deafness is always more of a handicap in the dark) Michael was returning to his Troop when his own sentry challenged him quietly. Michael did not hear and came on. The man slipped a round into his rifle and quietly challenged again, without reply. He had pulled back his safety catch before he suddenly detected who approached. 'I would rather shoot myself than harm Mr Pollock,' he told another subaltern, John North, a few weeks later.

At the end of April Colonel Draffen sent for Michael to say that he had regretfully decided to relieve him of his Troop and send him back to Egypt where a job at base would be arranged. Michael, of course, did not believe the deafness had worsened, 'but I do respect his decisions very considerably and feel certain he's right. For one has to think of other people as well as oneself and I do realise the things that *might* happen if I didn't hear just one word.' He was distressed beyond measure, however, at the thought of being sent far away to the safety of Cairo just before his beloved men would be involved in the biggest battle of the campaign. As Michael Halsted reflected, half a century later: 'That would have shaken his spirit; and the dear boy needed to remain and we needed him.'

Colonel Draffen did not, long afterwards, recall whether Michael entered a formal protest, but he pointed out that anyone ordered away from the Bays invariably protested! When Draffen himself, as a major early in the war, received orders to take up command of a yeomanry regiment, 'I even went to the War Office to protest but of course it was of no avail and rightly so. As I am sure you realise we were *always* an extremely happy Regiment and never wanted to leave it.'

The Colonel knew Michael's feelings and after reflection reprieved him and created a new post: Assistant to the Technical Adjutant, Major W. F. Lindley, whom Michael liked: 'a charming man who fought in the last war, used to keep a garage before this war, and is everybody's friend in the Regiment. There's nothing he doesn't know about engines.' The work should be unaffected by the deafness and Michael would serve with the Echelons, which had a vital role in any battle, and dangerous too, for the Echelons dashed about in trucks, lacking the armour of a tank.

'There's plenty of interest, and it's something new, something to give me a wider outlook. Although I don't like leaving my old work, I'm sure I'll get along all right with this and after all it was St Paul, I think, who said "I have learned in whatsoever state I am, therewith to be content."''

16

A Second Too Late

To cushion his sorrow at leaving the Troop, Michael's turn for leave came earlier than he had expected. The previous month he had written: 'I feel I could go on out here at this job for a year on end quite all right without leave. But I do know that when I do get it I shall enjoy it and I shall make the most of it as you can well imagine! Wouldn't it be *wonderful* if both Tom and I got our leave at the same time? I shall certainly have a shot at getting it like that, although it may not be easy.' Tom Butler-Stoney could not arrange it.

Early in May Michael left for the coast in the leave lorry. They transferred to railway cattle trucks at Bardia and then, after a night at Mersa Matruh transit camp, to comfortable carriages of the Egyptian State Railway. Michael watched from a window seat as the desert changed 'into fertile pastures, ploughland and the green trees of the Delta,' and so to Cairo after dark where Gordon Anthony, on leave earlier, had booked a room for Michael at the Mena House Hotel, at the foot of the Great Pyramid; the cooler air, country atmosphere and wide verandahs of Mena House were more enjoyable to Michael than the famous Shepheard's Hotel in the city.

'So I have my bath. What a luxury, after weeks of the desert. I'm afraid the valet will have a bit of scrubbing of the bath to do afterwards!' Then Michael went down to dinner beside the swimming pool. The next morning he began six days of sightseeing, including the Sphinx and the tunnels of the Great Pyramid; and of shopping and window shopping in the good stores and the crowded, colourful bazaars; and plenty of bathing in the hotel pool. Michael did not know many people in Cairo but through the Officers' Christian Union he met a cavalry major on the General Staff who gave him and two others lunch at the Gezira Club. While watching cricket afterwards from the verandah the major and Michael suddenly realised that they had met before: Major Kirkwood had taught mathematics at Charterhouse for one term, standing in for an absent master. 'We used to think him very funny and we were very naughty and used to unscrew the bolts of the desks to make them fall down!' Kirkwood is mentioned in one of the only two of the Charterhouse letters to survive: 'He is most frightfully nice and I think everybody likes him.' Kirkwood was later to be a good friend in need.

On the Sunday Michael attended the Cathedral and afterwards met the legendary Bishop Gwynne, who had gone to the Sudan as a missionary immediately after the reconquest in 1898, had been bishop since 1908, and during the First World War was summoned to France by Kitchener and the Chaplain-General to take charge of all chaplains on the Western Front. Michael also visited the Mission to Mediterranean Garrisons and saw over the English Mission School.

Many British girls were working in Cairo, whose

company was much enjoyed by servicemen, according to rank. Michael was not interested. At social occasions he was not shy but, like many boys of his generation from normal homes and British public schools, he developed slowly. When, a few weeks later, he had a cable announcing his elder brother's engagement, Michael was delighted, and joked that with two of the family 'fixed up' he would have to start looking around. Then he added: 'Thanks, but I would rather wait just now.' He probably would not have fallen in love and married until after the war.

Rather than dances, he went to the opera. His leave coincided with a gala performance of Rossini's *Barber of Seville* at the Royal Opera House: 'A great treat. Brilliantly acted and performed, and musically first class. The acting was superb – quite electric, especially the Barber himself. They played the Egyptian National Anthem at the beginning and the end. It's very short and quick and sounds rather like a practical joke, but perhaps ours does to other people!'

'Well, I did enjoy myself in Cairo,' Michael wrote on 13 May, back in the desert, where both sides were building up to launch their offensives. Michael immersed himself in his new duties while continuing to mess with 'A' Squadron and to be welfare officer. He went on a bathing expedition to the sea. 'We found a delightful little cove with a rocky road running down to it. There was a pleasant sandy beach, a gradual slope and then the incredible blue of the Mediterranean behind.'

It was a last jaunt before the dreadful days ahead.

On the evening of 26 May 1942 Rommel attacked the Gazala Line.

For the next nineteen days the Eighth Army fought

the battle known to historians as Gazala; to the troops it seemed a series of furious actions to which they gave names such as 'The Cauldron' or 'Knightsbridge' – a map identification point formed by a banner between two oil drums; Bir Hacheim was the well immortalised by the bravery of the Free French.

For the Queen's Bays the Battle of Gazala began when they counter-attacked south of Knightsbridge and threw back a German column which had by-passed Bir Hacheim; Colonel Draffen's brilliant handling earned him the DSO.

Gordon Anthony, Michael Halsted and Joe Radice were all wounded that morning and out of the fight, and five men were killed. The Bays covered themselves with glory. As Brigadier Briggs reminded them in his farewell a year later: 'Each day your Regiment fought one, two, three or even four major actions. There was no question of any rest; there was no question of any letting up at all. They were always moving here and there to wherever the fighting was heaviest.' The Adjutant, the Medical Officer and several other Bays received decorations.

Nobody in the Squadrons or the Echelons had much idea of the general course of a battle which covered an area thirty-five miles long and sixty deep, some two thousand square miles of desert. As the days of hard fighting wore on, the battlefield contracted and British losses exceeded the German. The 10th Hussars and 9th Lancers lost so many tanks that the Brigadier had to put them out of the line: only the Bays remained. Rommel began slowly to gain the upper hand.

'We rush backwards and forwards, with quite a lot to do,' wrote Michael during a pause on the third day of the battle. He and the Technical

Adjutant had 'a little truck to ourselves. Sleep is cut down a bit, but everybody is in the same boat about that.'

Lindley and Michael had to know the state of all tanks on the Regimental strength: how many were engaging the enemy, or undergoing repair in the front line, or back at the Light Aid Detachment where Captain Blain, a REME officer, supervised more serious repairs. Some had been sent farther back for major repair by Brigade or Divisional workshops and some were past recovery. The Colonel needed the information at any moment so that he, Brigadier Briggs and General Lumsden could know their exact strength when planning and executing movement and action. Lindley and Michael had to keep abreast of the spare parts state, obtained from the Technical Warrant Officer, John Wilson, and were responsible for the inspection and recovery of tanks shot up or broken down.

They were under shell fire occasionally – without the protection of a tank's armour – and were dive-bombed regularly. In the words of another Bays officer: 'The Stukas used to come in the late afternoon so they had the sun behind them, *i.e.* directly in our eyes, in "line ahead" formation and peel off one by one, diving straight down very low over our heads, drop their bombs and soar straight up into the sky and away. The RAF did the best they could to support us during these raids but they were very limited with the aircraft available, called Kittyhawks. The anti-aircraft defences were again only on a limited scale, and their task was made all the more difficult in shooting down the Stukas because of the sun.' Without the valiant efforts of the RAF in their American

Kittyhawks, the battle would have been lost much sooner.

On 12 June, the seventeenth day, Michael obtained the rare luxury of an air letter form and wrote home, for the cable had reached him, in the middle of the battle, which announced Martin's engagement to be married. After expressing his excitement and joy Michael continued: 'Out here we bowl along at a good rate; the weather is hot, but there's usually a cool wind to fan the temperature. As I write things are slightly inactive, really too much so for my liking. But it is giving me a chance to write you this. A few miles away there is much banging going on. At times, during the last week or so, things have been really lively, and often we lie down to sleep well after 12 and rise again soon after 5. It's a very good job I've got, although at present there's not too much to do and rather too much waiting. But we have interesting experiences and dash about in our little truck hither and thither.

'Sometimes we are by ourselves going from one formation to another. Other times, we take our place in the supply convoy and rattle along over the sometimes very bumpy ground. It would remind Martin of the sea, to see all these vehicles one after another pushing up the dust in front of them, just like the ocean convoy in which we or anyone else came out here.

'Very often at night time we ourselves push up to the front line and spend the night with the tanks. This is what I like doing and especially being able to go over and talk with the old Squadron. Often we bring up food or drink or newspapers, and usually take back the letters for home and (sometimes) the dirty washing!! Then we may glide out in the first light of the morning and wend our way back to the 2nd Line. A little breakfast is always a pleasant event, and after that we may very likely go farther back still and fix up one or two things for the Regiment and see to one or two vehicles . . . Further behind the front line we can occasionally drop into the Mess there and this is a nice change from our own cooking efforts. (In actual fact, the corporal on our truck is an excellent cook and a *very* good maker of tea.)'

Michael managed one air letter to me, written in snatches between 7 and 11 June, the period when the Free French were defending Bir Hacheim, to the south of the Bays. Parts of the letter concern the family or my affairs, but the rest reveals a sensitive Christian unburdening himself: 'Today is Sunday,' he began, 'although you would hardly know it as everything is the same bustle and really I suppose it is difficult to have a day's rest with a war going on. There's no reason, however, why one shouldn't remember the day. It does seem somehow that the guns have quietened a bit and perhaps the Germans too, in their heart of hearts, respect the only real God . . .

'You may rest assured that this Regiment is playing a valuable part in the defeat of the common enemy, and it would thrill you to see the real earnest cheerfulness and enthusiasm that is being shown by everyone in the great effort we are making to finish it off and so be able to leave the desert.'

The 2nd Armoured Brigade was, in fact, fighting

brilliantly and no subaltern is anything but an optimist; but the Eighth Army was being rapidly out-generalled. Even as Michael wrote, Rommel had regrouped and was bringing up fresh supplies, ready for the assault which would indeed make the British 'leave the desert', or at least the Libyan desert, in a way Michael did not mean.

He continued: 'I had a shock today when I heard that a charming man who used to be in my Troop and was my own tank's operator was killed the other day. He was really one of the best and I've known him ever since he joined the Regiment. Certainly out here, he and I have shared plenty of enjoyments and excitements, and there must have been few things which we never discussed. Alas, however, the most important of all things, his soul, we never discussed. It was my fault, but somehow I just never got started. He knew, of course, that I had very definite beliefs about these things but apart from that I hardly explained things to him. He always used to go to Holy Communion and morning services as often as possible, but what exactly he believed when he died, I cannot tell. No doubt you understand my feelings, but I don't think I can do much else about it except pray.'

This touches again on Michael's dilemma. His conviction about immortality, and of the truth of Christ's saying, 'No man cometh to the Father but by me,' gave him a sense of mission towards those around him. He knew that religious habits were not in themselves enough; that though he himself had always been Godfearing it was not until that day on Salisbury Plain in October 1940 that he had 'passed from death unto life'. Yet he shrank from probing into the private recesses of his friends' minds. On hearing of Trooper Foster's death, Michael could think only that he had not discharged his Christian duty.

He could not know, until they met again, how in the horrors of war his unashamed faith and his leadership had sustained and encouraged a young disciple of Christ.

Michael next described events in a few guarded lines and then gave me a passage which shines down the years: 'Things have been busy and often I find it difficult to concentrate even though sometimes we may have a decent period of doing nothing. I ought to be able to solve this problem, however, by persevering and I feel that even though there are times when one just doesn't think of praying *those* are the best occasions to do so. This life out here gives the Devil and his works great opportunities. Day after day flies by and one finds something to do from the moment one rises (often in the dark) to bedtime (always also in the dark). Therefore, for reading, the only time is in the daytime, and naturally this isn't always possible. But chances are often there but I may miss them because I'm thinking too much of other things.

'But the Lord is, of course, as ever the kind Shepherd who will whisper in my ear what He wants me to hear, and after all, "My grace is sufficient for thee." Sometimes the best time of the day is just that short period when I'm lying down, about to go to sleep. Too often I fall asleep almost immediately, but other times I gaze at the stars and meditate upon the wonders of this universe – all made by His hand.'

*

Discomforts, dangers and the unknown future in a battle which grew daily more hectic, were overridden by the Shepherd's presence and friendship. In an earlier letter, after I had won my scholarship and gone up at once to Cambridge, Michael rejoiced that things were going well for me, 'as of course they're bound to go wherever you are, with a Friend such as you've got'. As he wrote to one of the hospitable old ladies of Farnham: 'When you are sitting in the desert, with the dust and the wind and the hot sun, the inside knowledge that you are being cared for every minute of the day and night by the Blessed Lord Himself, makes life really worth living.'

At dawn on Saturday 13 June the remaining tanks of the Bays took up position as an advanced armoured screen protecting the Knightsbridge Box, a feature well dug, wired and mined, defended by 201 Guards Brigade. At first light a heavy German attack came in, outnumbering the Bays by four tanks to one. The battle was furious and by 8 a.m. petrol and ammunition were running short, for supplies had not come up since the previous midday from the Brigade's massed Echelons, positioned about twelve miles north of Knightsbridge on a plateau beneath a low escarpment, a little north-east of Acroma, west of Tobruk; their every attempt to send supplies had failed because the Germans had won almost complete mastery of the air.

At 8.45 a.m. Colonel Draffen had to pull back the Regiment about half a mile to secure their flank on a minefield. An hour later they were relieved by a tank brigade and withdrew some miles north to get food and replenishment and to rest. They were reduced to twelve tanks.

When Lindley and Michael, waiting in the Echelon, heard the news from their wireless operator, they and their technical staff and the vital supplies set out south to go to the Regiment. The short drive was interrupted by air raids, when they all had to leap from their trucks for cover. It was in one of these raids that Michael saw his former Troop Sergeant, Clare, and a corporal killed before his eyes. The rest got through, and the crews of damaged tanks were encouraged by Lindley's calm efficiency and Michael's cheerful smile as they did what they could, their faces streaked with oil and sweat and their shirts and shorts camouflaged inevitably with sand.

The noise of gunfire to the south died down until about 2 p.m., when the Regiment was ordered west to help the Scots Guards. As the remaining tanks, their crews weary but in fine heart, trundled off to renew the battle, Michael and the other officers and men of the Echelons withdrew north, passing through a sandstorm which reduced visibility to two hundred yards.

By now the German armour, despite heavy casualties, had the whiphand, so that the British Official War History labels these June days as 'the Defeat of the British Armour'. About 6 p.m. the forward companies of the Scots Guards were overrun and the Bays had to withdraw on one flank to protect the Guards' battalion headquarters. The fight continued but an order for general withdrawal, to ensure the defence of the Acroma Gap and Tobruk, could not be long delayed.

Back with the Echelons on the plateau beneath the escarpment, air raids were too common to be recorded. Slit trenches had been dug and work stopped only briefly. For Michael, with his tendency to deafness, the bomb explosions and the anti-aircraft fire increased the strain on ears already weakened by fatigue: his reactions were retarded by a vital split-second or more.

Shortly before sunset Michael and six or seven other officers began to eat supper at a table laid beside the Mess lorry. Peter Willett was one of them, his tank having been lost by mechanical breakdown.

Suddenly yet another formation of fighter bombers came low over the escarpment. The Stukas flew out of the setting sun to give the least possible warning. At the sound of the aircraft the officers jumped up from the table to dive into the nearest slit trenches, 'but Michael,' writes Peter Willett, 'must have heard the planes just a second later than the rest of us and was caught before he could reach a slit trench, though he had left the table.'

When the smoke and sand cleared away the others saw Michael lying unconscious and dashed towards him. The bomb had not landed very near; he had been hit by a splinter between the left eye and his steel helmet and knocked out: a second later he would have been safe.

When stretcher bearers gave first aid and carried him to an ambulance the gash on his head did not look too bad.

17

The End of the Beginning

Michael recovered consciousness two days later.

By then the Battle of Gazala was over. Throughout Sunday 14 June the ten remaining Bays' tanks, with supporting guns and 1st Battalion Rifle Brigade, had held the Acroma Gap. Under heavy fire and frequent assault, undefeated, they fought until the whole 13th Army Corps withdrew in the early hours of 15 June. When the Bays were ordered to hand over their few last tanks and evacuate by lorry, no armoured regiment had been in continuous action so long.

Since Gordon Anthony had been severely wounded in the knee, only Douglas MacCallan remained of the three Old Carthusians who had joined the Queen's Bays together. Douglas fought right through to 1945 unscathed, except for a graze, by shot, shell or bomb.

The bomb splinter had been removed from Michael's skull within a few hours, for the Eighth Army's medical services in the field were highly organised. On Sunday 21 June, only eight days after he was hit, he was brought into the great 15th (Scottish) General Hospital on the outskirts of Cairo. A fractured skull does not encourage too lively an interest in the world; Michael lay thankful to be alive, with the gash healing fast even if the shaving of the entire left side of his head made a peculiar and amusing reflection in a mirror. He was also much deafer, though hardly aware of it.

His first thought on arriving at Cairo was to cable home to relieve the anxiety caused by the War Office telegram which would have reported him wounded. He had to use the number-code. This method allowed only a choice of set phrases which were cabled to Britain by number. Michael's message read: '*All well and safe. My thoughts are with you. Loving greetings.*'

It arrived on 4 July – and brought far more relief than he could have expected.

For when he had been X-rayed, immediately on arrival at 15th Scottish Hospital, the plates revealed, in the words of the subsequent medical report, that 'the injury was more severe than would be imagined by external appearances'. The bomb metal which had fractured the skull had created a rare but extremely dangerous condition: it had opened a gap from the brain to the back of the nose, and the occasional 'runny nose' which Michael noticed and discounted was not a form of common cold, as he supposed, but fluid from the brain itself. If fluid can get out of the brain, germs can get in. Unless the gap closed, fatal meningitis would develop sooner or later.

The surgeons decided to allow six weeks to build up Michael's strength and then, if the gap had not closed on its own, they must perform a difficult and dangerous operation to save his life. Unknown to Michael, who felt better every day, he was at once placed on the dangerously ill list.

The War Office telegram, 'Wounded in action on 13 June' reached my parents on 29 June. When a second

telegram three days later said he was on the Danger
List we naturally supposed that Michael hung between
life and death. In another two days came his cheerful
cable. We all assumed he had turned the corner. There
was nothing to warn us to the contrary because the War
Office telegrams showed no Middle East date-line, and
we could not know that the hospital had placed him on
the Danger List the very day he cabled.

Michael was as ignorant of his danger as we. By
the last day of June he felt well enough to start an
air mail letter home, though it took him several days
to complete. On 2 July, the day the 'dangerously ill'
telegram reached us in England, he laid the letter aside
to write an airgraph which would get home very much
quicker than an air mail letter. The airgraph allayed
our anxieties completely. The writing was clear, and
he wrote: 'The injury wasn't particularly bad and has
in fact already healed up. I suffered no pain at all as I
was knocked out straightaway! . . . I am extremely well
looked after and am having a very nice rest.'

The 15th Scottish had the reputation of being the finest
hospital in the Middle East. The modern, brick-built
Agousa Hospital on the banks of the Nile had been
requisitioned early in the war and was staffed by
first-class teams of surgeons, doctors and nurses.
The surgeon in charge of Michael's case, Major Peter
Ashcroft, aged forty, was professor of neuro-surgery at
the Middlesex Hospital and world famous in medical
circles. Lord Richardson, who the next year was his
opposite number as head of the medical side when
Ashcroft, on promotion, became head of the surgical
side in the main military hospital in Algiers, says that
in 1942 he was at the peak of his powers. Slim and of

medium height, with dark hair, he had an easy and kindly manner. Michael could not have been in better hands.

He was in a two-bed ward with one other officer. On 4 July he wrote: 'It's an extremely nice room with all the modern fitings and attachments, and French windows out on to a balcony. Beyond the balcony there's quite a pleasant view, the best part of which (to me) is the large number of trees, which of course we never see in the desert. A main road runs along on the right, and while I am eating my breakfast in the morning I can see the white tramcars speeding by, full of passengers going to work. There's luckily a continual breeze blowing through the room so that it seldom if ever gets really hot.'

The city itself was stifling in July. However, 'The nurses are most helpful and full of good humour,' the food was excellent, with plenty of fresh fruit, and he was looking forward to getting up. Colonel Tom Draffen visited 15th Scottish on 6 July (as he recorded in his diary) 'to see Michael Halsted (he lost an eye) and Michael Pollock. Both very cheery.' Many years later Colonel Tom could 'remember quite clearly the Sister telling me they should both be out before long'.

Michael began to read again. Letters from home arrived fast; the newspaper came with his breakfast, instead of weeks late as in the desert. He had plenty of visitors. The Eighth Army having withdrawn to the Alamein Line, day-leaves to Cairo had enabled the Colonel and others to look in, while Bays serving on the General Staff made a point of visiting the Regiment's wounded. The hospital chaplain, L. S. Cuthbert, became a good friend, and on Michael mentioning that he belonged to the Officers' Christian

Union, Cuthbert told another member, Major L. H. Milligan, a radiologist at the hospital. Dr Milligan took the trouble to call in almost every day to chat with Michael and his companion, though professional ward visits were not part of his duty. He wrote afterwards to me of Michael's 'inspiring friendship, courage and devotion to his Master . . . I came to look forward with great pleasure to my visit, both of us, I believe, feeling the bond of love through our Heavenly Father.'

By 11 July, exactly four weeks after he was hit, Michael was at last '. . . *up* and walking about (although slightly weakly at present!) and trying to accustom myself to more normal ways of living than lying in bed! I should consider myself lucky not to have been double or treble my period in bed, as many people must have been before now. But as it is I'm hoping my legs will get strong as soon as possible and I shall be once more able to run and do P.T. and play football – or rather cricket, it should be by now, I think.'

He was already discussing future prospects. He expected to go to a convalescent home and then rejoin the Regiment.

Alex Barclay was now second-in-command; on Tom Draffen's promotion soon afterwards, Barclay became the Colonel, and led the Bays right through to Tunis, with Ermyntrude, who won much admiration from the French. Alex Barclay 'suddenly pounced in and wanted to know if all was well. You can guess how extremely pleasant it is to see anybody like that and how much it brightens things up.' To Draffen, Barclay and any other visitor it was clear that Michael's increased deafness made return to the Regiment unlikely, though they did not say so. They rejoiced that evidently he would leave hospital soon.

That Sunday, 12 July, he was able to go down to the chapel on the floor below for the morning service and afterwards he received another batch of letters from home. He would get up soon after breakfast and, before the day became too hot, sit on the balcony, from where he could see the Nile.

However, by the end of the week he was back in bed. Further X-rays showed that the split in his skull had not closed at all. The doctors hid their concern from Michael though they seem to have mentioned, with cheerful casualness, that they might need to operate again to remove 'a few small foreign bodies which are still inside'. Michael began to feel a headache and lost both his appetite and sense of smell. 'I've never had a headache like it,' he wrote on 20 July. 'Nor have I ever had a headache that went on for such a long time.' It was his one discouraged remark in the entire correspondence, and he added at once: 'But really you can be sure that it is much of a muchness and nothing very serious. It doesn't prevent me sleeping or eating or waking or reading; it doesn't make me sleep walk or sleep talk or generally be a nuisance! It doesn't, in fact, worry me much.'

But it did, far more than he wanted anyone to realise. The doctors and nurses knew only from their professional observations what Michael was suffering. 'Your son was a magnificent patient,' wrote Ashcroft. 'He never complained, he was universally admired and loved by all the nurses, patients and doctors who came in contact with him. In circumstances of this kind one sees the best and the worst in a man. No praise can be too high for Michael Pollock.'

His character came to its fruition. Michael was fulfilling the role given to disciples in one of his favourite Bible verses: 'Let your light so shine before men that they may . . . glorify your Father which is in heaven' (Matthew 5:16). Michael loved that word 'shine', as when St Paul wrote: 'Ye shine as lights in the world; holding forth the word of life' (Philippians 2: 15–16) or, 'God . . . hath shined in our hearts, to give the light of the knowledge of the glory of God in the face of Jesus Christ' (2 Corinthians 4: 6). Michael would sometimes sign off his letters to me with the phrase: 'Keep shining'. But whereas some Christians shine artificially, hoping that the dazzle will blind their neighbours to the self-will or irritability beneath the bland surface, Michael was just being himself, refashioned by the grace of God. He loved to make others happy, and hoped he might help them to see that Jesus Christ was the best Friend for anyone. Tom Butler-Stoney, who came in whenever he could, wrote to Michael's parents afterwards: 'From the talks I had with him I know that the Lord Jesus was very close.'

Tom Butler-Stoney had been briefly in hospital himself with a shell splinter in the calf of his leg. At his first visit on 22 July he thought Michael 'pretty bad but extremely cheerful'. At each of his next two visits Michael seemed to be improving, and by the last days of July he was up again for a few hours. Michael reported in a letter home less headache, but 'I've got rather a comic runny nose – only in one nostril! When I sit up it runs, when I lie down it stops. I lie down as much as possible! My doctor thinks it rather amusing . . .' Aschroft did not, of course, think it amusing, at all. He took a very grave view of the case when this 'leak of fluid from the brain became more copious. There was nothing for it but to operate again.'

On 1 August, not knowing he had less than four

days to live, Michael wrote me an air letter. He chatted about home and our friends and my plans, and told me of Major Milligan, Major Kirkwood and other frequent visitors. He wrote that he was now reading St Paul's First Epistle to Timothy and studying *100 Days*, the popular book of Bible studies prepared specially for officers some eighteen years before by Major Arthur Smith of the Coldstream Guards, who became Wavell's Chief of Staff in the Middle East and afterwards commander-in-chief in India. Michael was beginning with the portions on the Holy Spirit.

He went on: 'It's wonderful you know, I've been here six weeks tomorrow but don't feel in the slightest bored – although of course wanting to be back with the Regiment. I find plenty to do, but please pray that now and always I use my time well – "To the Lord, and not unto men." Also please pray that I may get to know more of the Bible, as I feel that my knowledge at present isn't very extensive, although of course the more I read (with prayer) the more presumably I shall learn . . .'

Winston Churchill was flying towards Cairo on Monday 3 August for the vital discussions which brought Alexander and Montgomery to the Desert War and prepared the way for the victory of Alamein. A mere subaltern knew nothing of this top-secret flight. Michael spent considerable time this last full day of his life writing a long air letter home.

He crowded into the three sides of the form a total of no less than a hundred and four lines, small but very straight and clear, running to more than a thousand words. They concerned nothing in particular for there seemed nothing in particular to report, but for a young man of twenty-two to compose such an interesting letter, much of it being amusing comment on family and local news which my parents had sent him, suggests that whatever his other achievements, had he lived, he might have been known as a writer.

He wrote: 'I am sorry you can't both be with me and have tea on my balcony. You could sit and admire the various types of barge with their huge masts plying up and down the Nile, or you could gaze across the green fields and palm trees at the pink line of hills away in the distance. Someone is banging with a hammer over there, as a new hut is put up in the hospital grounds: away on the path by the road, an Arab walks by – carrying a sunshade! Funnily enough you don't see many of those handy implements out here . . .

'I'm afraid I'm coming to the end of my space. I'm sorry this letter hasn't contained very much other than rubbish! It must be the "staying in bed" atmosphere that has me.

'I hope you are beginning to get my letters from here now. They will tell you all is going well. Please give my Love to All, and thank you again for your letters. Very Best Love – *Michael*.'

When he finished these last words he probably did not know that his operation would be the next day. He knew by the evening. Major Milligan wrote of the 'gallant confidence with which that happy laddie faced the pain and trials associated with his wounds. The evening before his operation he was the same smiling, content patient ready to do his duty.'

Next morning, so Sister Evelyn White told my parents, 'He went to this operation straight from his usual habit of Bible reading and communion with God. He went happy and confident.'

His devotions generally began with a reading of *Daily Light*. The text for the morning of 4 August is: 'It is finished: and he bowed his head, and gave up the ghost.' The entire meditation concerns the death of 'Jesus, the author and finisher of our faith,' and includes such words of Christ as: 'I have glorified thee on the earth: I have finished the work which thou gavest me to do,' and, 'We are sanctified through the offering of the body of Jesus Christ once for all.'

The meditation ends: 'Greater love hath no man than this, that a man lay down his life for his friends.' The friendship of Christ had been Michael's mainspring. Because of it he had no fear of death. Tom Butler-Stoney stressed this to me afterwards. Tom had no fear either, and when he was killed instantly on the Mareth Line seven months later, his death meant simply what he had said of Michael's, that he had 'gone on ahead of us to live with the Lord'.

Michael did not expect to die. When wheeled into the theatre he had no idea that the operation would be dangerous and technically difficult, nor that it gave the sole hope of avoiding death from meningitis, nor that his brain had sustained considerably more damage than earlier X-rays had shown. But I am very sure that his last conscious thoughts before the anaesthetic were peaceful and content: he would have been inwardly talking to the Lord Jesus.

Ashcroft closed the gap in the skull with less difficulty than expected. But just as he finished, Michael's breathing became affected and then ceased. They began artificial respiration. For eight hours, all through that 4 August 1942 when, a few miles away, Churchill and his generals were reshaping the war, a surgical team fought for the life of a subaltern.

At last Michael began to breathe again, fitfully. The surgeons hoped to re-establish the breathing 'but the strain must have been too great,' runs Aschroft's report, 'for after some time, in spite of the aid of oxygen and injection of powerful substances to stimulate breathing, he began to fail and passed away peacefully at a quarter past nine without regaining consciousness.'

Three weeks later, several days after the telegram announcing his death, his last letter reached me.

It ended: 'Space is getting short. Thank you again, John, for all your wonderful letters and cards, and your prayers. I'm progressing well and with His help I shall soon be out and about again – a fit man! Remember me to all. I'll write again. All my love.'

After the signature in the tiny space remaining on the air letter form, he added: ' "Oh that men would praise the Lord for his goodness"!'

So he passed over,
and all the trumpets sounded for him
on the other side.